P.U.R.S.E.S.

A Practical and Complete Guide to
Financial Security for Every Woman

Bobbie Messmore

Order this book online at www.thejewels.org

Order this book online at www.trafford.com
or email orders@trafford.com

Most Trafford titles are also available at major online book retailers.

Printed in the United States of America.

ISBN: 978-1-4907-4281-6 (sc)
ISBN: 978-1-4907-4283-0 (hc)
ISBN: 978-1-4907-4282-3 (e)

Library of Congress Control Number: 2014913428

Trafford rev. 09/30/2014

 www.trafford.com

North America & international
toll-free: 1 888 232 4444 (USA & Canada)
fax: 812 355 4082

CONTENTS

ACKNOWLEDGMENTS

This book has been a dream of mine for quite some time. Once I gave myself a deadline, it finally became a reality. Many people have been a part of helping this dream come true. First, I want to thank my amazing family for their love, encouragement and constant support. My husband, Thomas, has offered a steady stream of understanding and flexibility to accommodate the time and effort required of me to complete such a project. He has been my biggest fan, cheering me along as I followed my passion to write. I also want to acknowledge my three sons, Brad, Jason and Matthew, who have all been involved in our family business over the years. They are successful young men who have not only shown love and care for me as their mother, but also respect for my business efforts and personal goals and dreams.

Next, I want to acknowledge my awesome employees, especially Cheryl, my personal assistant. Thank you, Cheryl, for overseeing the day-to-day tasks in the company while I focused on completing this book. Having you by my side over the past several years has meant so much to me.

And last, but certainly not least, I want to thank my best friend, Jolie. Not only did she design the cute purses that appear throughout the chapters of this book, but she has been the most wonderful friend a girl could ever hope for. Thank you, Jolie, for being there in the good times, the hard times and everywhere in between.

INTRODUCTION

Sitting at their favorite restaurant on Madison Avenue in Manhattan, Susan and Marie were enjoying a delightful lunch on a perfect summer's day. As usual, they chatted about fashion, relationships and their busy schedules. Marie was excited about the new outfit she had just purchased and shared with Susan the details of the event at which it would be worn. She also updated Susan on the new relationship that was developing between herself and the man of her dreams.

Susan had something else on her mind. She had taken quite an interest in learning about finances. She had recently read some books on the subject, as well as attended a financial seminar that had been held in her area. Susan began to share with Marie the details of what she had learned. Then she asked Marie, "Why do you think so many women seem unconcerned about their finances? Do you think it's ignorance or apathy?"

Marie leaned forward, looked straight into Susan's eyes and said, "I don't know and I don't care."

While this is a fictitious and somewhat humorous story, there is much truth to be gleaned from the two women's very different views on financial planning. Some women take aggressive steps to participate in their own financial security. Statistics on female college graduates, executives and business owners are more impressive than ever. Women, who at one time sat silently while their husbands and financial advisers discussed their portfolios, are now taking on a more active role in meetings and are becoming far more involved in decision making.

On the other hand, there are still untold thousands of women everywhere who do not understand the importance of becoming an active participant in their own financial future. Many of these women take Marie's approach: "I don't know and I don't care." Others do care, but the thought of putting together a financial plan is overwhelming; they don't know where to start. And then there are the procrastinators who live on Someday Isle—some day I'll do this; some day I'll do that. These ladies do not deal with financial matters until a crisis forces an extreme sense of urgency. One example of this is the sudden loss of a spouse due to death or divorce. Not only are these women dealing with the emotions of highly stressful, traumatic events, having the added pressure of mapping out a financial future for themselves can be overwhelming.

As a financial professional who has spoken to thousands of women one-on-one or from the platform during a seminar, I have encountered women of every type. There are those who are financially savvy, very successful and take the bull by the horns when dealing with their portfolios. I have also met women who have jobs that provide a steady paycheck but have no idea how to plan for retirement. Many retired women wonder if they will have enough money to see them through to the end of their lives. Some women tell me that they have never even written a check because their husbands had always handled everything regarding finances.

Many women don't know the difference between a mutual fund and a mutual friend. By no means does this indicate ignorance; it simply means that they have never learned much about financial matters. Over the years, I have met with extremely well-educated people, many of whom hold master's degrees or doctorates. While they are very knowledgeable in their fields of expertise, the notion of dealing with a financial portfolio seems very intimidating to them.

This really is not that shocking to me. When you stop to think about it, how much training on the subject of finances do we really get during our educational years? You would think that offering classes to students on money, budgets, and saving for retirement would be a priority. While it is critical to train students on how to earn a living, shouldn't they also be trained on how to manage their earnings? I mention this not to debate the educational system but rather to help us understand why many people feel ill-equipped when it comes to building a solid portfolio.

You may wonder what all of this has to do with "purses." As you will see in chapter one, P.U.R.S.E.S. is an acronym. Each letter begins a phrase that represents a key element pertinent to designing a strong financial plan, one that will endure the test of time.

This book offers no advice on which stocks or mutual funds one should invest in. You will not come across complicated language and confusing calculations. What you will find is a clear and concise roadmap that can help lead you to that special place of financial security every woman longs for. The road is not meant to be traveled alone. You may likely still need the services of professionals such as financial advisers, CPAs or attorneys. But knowing the right questions to ask those professionals and being able to understand their various recommendations will be priceless. You will be equipped to make good decisions.

Just as women have many different tastes in purses—color, size and style—they also have different situations that will require them to build a financial plan that is unique to them. No two women are exactly alike; they have different assets, incomes, family structures, etc. Each one should build a plan that encompasses her individual needs and circumstances.

Financial planning is no longer just a subject for men. It's been said of Ginger Rogers that she did everything Fred Astaire did "backwards…. and in high heels!" Be a confident woman today and begin your journey to a lifetime of financial security!

PART I

Money: Facts, Fiction, Focus

CHAPTER 1

P.U.R.S.E.S.

Most women, if not every woman, are in possession of one or more purses. No matter where you go, if there are women around, chances are you will see many varieties of purses. Styles, colors and designer names are normally a reflection of the lady carrying the purse. Some women prefer subtle classic styles, while others go for a more flamboyant look.

Purses have been around for thousands of years. Their initial purpose was to carry money. Over the years, purses have evolved into everything from a fashion statement to a functional miniature suitcase. When choosing a purse, most women initially are drawn to how the purse looks on the outside. Normally, when a lady is scanning hundreds of purses in a department store, certain purses jump out and capture her attention. An immediate bond is formed between the purse and the woman, as if it has called out to her by name. She cannot imagine leaving this newfound friend behind.

For some, the exterior of the purse is all that matters. How they will be perceived when carrying the purse is of the utmost importance to them. Does it have the right designer name, is it the latest version, will the purse "pop" with the outfit it is intended to accessorize? The woman envisions herself walking into a party carrying the prize in her hand.

Many women have a financial planner,
but most do not have a financial plan.

For others, functionality is critical when choosing a purse. These women immediately look inside to evaluate roominess, numbers of compartments, accessibility for a cell phone, keys or lipstick. Will it accommodate a baby bottle and diaper, therefore doubling as a diaper bag?

Whatever the reason for selecting a particular purse, one thing is certain: it is a very personal decision. Whether the purse was chosen for its appearance, functionality or a combination of the two, a purse plays an important and valuable role in the life of a woman.

In addition, a purse makes a woman feel secure in a lot of ways. Before leaving home, most women open their purses to make sure they have everything they need inside. A woman's checklist normally consists of things such as money, credit cards, glasses, lipstick and cell phone. Having these items safely tucked away and by her side can give her a sense of security. She knows she has all of the essential items she may need at any given time and can get through almost any situation with these necessities.

From that perspective, let's examine the acronym P.U.R.S.E.S. When related to financial issues, a woman should have a personal financial plan that consists of all the items needed to carry her though any of life's circumstances. A good financial plan will result in a woman feeling safe, secure and confident.

Purpose Based Planning

Women are notorious for planning things. We spend untold hours, days, weeks and sometimes even months planning for everything from our daily tasks and schedules to various special occasions and events. Our planning revolves around a *purpose*, an intended or desired result.

Just think about all of the different types of things a woman plans for during her lifetime.

We go to great lengths to plan our outfit for an upcoming special occasion. We spend hours upon hours shopping, maneuvering in and out of stores, trying on numerous articles of clothing. Then we look for the perfect pieces of jewelry and try on every make and model of shoes. And, of course, we must seek out that special pocketbook that will complete a perfectly coordinated outfit. From our teenage years, preparing to attend the prom, to deciding what we will wear to our twenty-fifth class reunion, an upcoming dinner party, weddings, funerals, and everything in between, we are very serious and determined about making sure we have done our due diligence to put together the perfect ensemble, one that is the product of a well-thought-out, many times labor-intensive process.

We plan our wedding, giving special attention to every little detail. We spend time choosing our colors, our dress as well as the attendants', our flowers, our photographer, our venue, our guest list, our invitation, our reception, our cake and our honeymoon.

In choosing a home to live in, we rarely make a decision after very little deliberation. No, the truth is that we consider everything about the home: the location, price, style, features and amenities. Many times we seek the advice of a realtor to help us understand our many options and assist us in comparing the advantages of limitless possibilities. Before making our decision, we trudge through house after house, making sure we have completed a thorough investigation of every conceivable choice.

Once the decision has been made, we embark on an endless journey of planning decorations and furniture placement that will maximize the beauty and functionality of the home.

We plan for children. Even though we sometimes get an unexpected surprise, most of the time we plan when and how many children we will have. When they arrive, an entirely new world of planning is put into motion. From our children's birth until they reach adulthood, we are constantly involved in putting together schedules for them that include everything from naps to curfews, homework time to soccer practice, birthday parties to graduation. We become geniuses at coordinating a plan that keeps what sometimes may seem to be a thousand balls in the air at one time.

Women spend enormous amounts of time planning for holidays—shopping, decorating and coordinating special meals. Let's consider one holiday most people can relate to: Christmas. The reason for the season is the celebration of the birth of Christ, but, that being said, it is also a special time for giving and spending time with friends and family. Because of the nurturing nature of women, we will put a great deal of time, money and effort into making this holiday a memorable experience for those we love. Why else would we spend weeks and even months making gift lists, shopping endlessly in congested malls, standing in never-ending lines at the checkout, decorating, wrapping gifts and cooking meals that literally cannot be completed in only one day? In order to create the ambience we want to provide for the ones we love, we must be fantastic planners to pull everything off.

Think about all of these many, many things we spend time planning. Our entire lives as women are full of them. But most women spend very little time or effort planning for an extremely important aspect of their lives: their financial future, financial stability and financial security. While there are some women who have done a tremendous job putting together a financial plan, the majority of us do not take this part of life seriously enough.

Many women have a *financial planner*, but most do not have a *financial plan.* Just having a mixture of investments does not indicate any type of Purpose Based Plan. Picking investments without a plan is like picking ingredients off the grocery store shelf with no idea what recipe you plan to use them for. A true financial plan has a *defined purpose* and a desired end result.

Over the years, I have met with hundreds of women to discuss their financial plans. Usually, when I inquire what their particular assets are to be used for, they cannot tell me. I get answers such as, "I'm not sure; I've just been saving," or "My friend told me this is the investment she chose, so I just put some money there as well." Very seldom do I hear about a well-thought-out plan.

That type of planning is really no plan at all. Operating in this manner is like driving a car without having a destination in mind, or gathering building materials without having any idea what you intend to build.

Every woman should take the time to consider and discover what type of plan she needs in order to meet her particular situation. I have never met any two people who had the exact same assets, family structure and financial goals. Everyone is unique; therefore financial planning should be designed to meet the particular needs of each individual. In chapter seven, we will explore strong Purpose Based Plans that work.

Understanding Money Basics

While it isn't necessary for every woman to have a degree in finance, it would serve them well to have a basic understanding of money. Most people know how to make money, but they do not know how to make money work for them. Women tend to look at today's money: How much do I have right now? How much can I spend today?

To be financially secure, women must take on the responsibility of planning for the future. When a woman is married, this task typically has been left to her spouse, although there are certainly some women who are very involved with their families' finances.

So many times, I have met with widows who have come to me for financial guidance and/or estate planning soon after the loss of their spouses. They are in a place I respectfully call Widow Wonderland. Not only are they going through a very difficult time as a result of their recent loss, they are beginning to wonder about many things. Widows wonder how they will make it without the involvement of their husbands' financial decision-making prowess. They wonder if there will be enough money for them to live on with the loss or reduction of their husbands' pension. When both spouses are drawing social security checks and one ends at the husband's death, a widow will wonder how impactful this will be to her financial security.

Some of these ladies never had any involvement in the financial planning aspect of her marriage. The extent of her financial responsibility was managing the allotment she received from her spouse for household expenses. Most men who pass away leaving their wives ill-equipped to handle finances never meant to put a burden on them. Normally, these men were trying to do the admirable thing of being the provider for their family taking any burden or concern off the shoulders of their wives by carrying the load themselves. Unfortunately, as a result of this good intention, many women are left without the basic skills and knowledge to manage their finances on their own.

Today, more and more women, along with their husbands, are beginning to understand the importance of both spouses being involved with the finances of their family. Even if one has a job and the other doesn't, or only one handles most of the financial transactions, it is still imperative that both spouses are aware and informed of their finances, investments and asset management. After reading this book, you should have a basic understanding of all of these things.

Resources Available

Women should also have some knowledge of the resources available to them for planning their financial portfolio. To keep things simple, let's just look at the basics regarding this issue. There are three primary providers of our accounts: banks, brokerage firms and insurance companies. Each specializes in certain areas, although these days there are so many crossovers that it's sometimes hard to tell who does what. But for the most part, we look to them for specific purposes.

The first institution is the bank. We most commonly use banks for checking accounts, savings accounts, money market accounts and certificates of deposit (CDs). Based on our short-term and long-term needs, we determine which of these types of accounts are best for us.

Next we come to the brokerage firm. The most common investments provided by these firms are stocks, bonds and mutual funds. Based on the type of firm you choose, a person may be more personally responsible for picking her own investments as opposed to using one particular brokerage firm representative to handle the management of the portfolio.

Lastly, an insurance company is the supplier of such products as life insurance, annuities and long-term care policies.

Based on your individual needs, goals and risk tolerance, you should be able to use the ten tools just mentioned—checking accounts, savings accounts, money market accounts, CDs, stocks, bonds, mutual funds, life insurance, annuities and long-term care policies—to build the financial portfolio that best fits your situation. Of course there are other investment choices such as real estate and business ownership. Greater detail regarding all of these various accounts, investments and products will be discussed in the chapters that follow.

Having the right combination of these tools is paramount. Many problems can occur when a portfolio does not include the right mixture. As you move through the different stages of life, chances are your needs will change. Very seldom does the portfolio of a thirty-two-year-old woman closely resemble that of someone who is sixty-eight.

The winning combination is the one that works for you. As you pursue Purpose Based Planning, you will realize the importance of choosing correctly. Many retired women are extremely frustrated with their current choices. This is mainly due to having a portfolio that in no way reflects a strategy that fits her particular needs.

There are many components that must be considered when choosing the appropriate resources, such as income needs for the present as well as the future, tax planning, insurance needs, etc. Without a well-thought-out Purpose Based Plan, the right combination may never be discovered, resulting in a portfolio that does not meet the needs of the individual.

Stages of Life

As we move through the various stages of life, we must continually adapt our finances. When our finances are out of sync with our particular stage of life, a calamity can occur.

There are four basic financial stages of life, some of which may be experienced simultaneously. As women enter middle age and beyond, some of the stages will take on a higher priority than they did in the past.

Stage #1: Accumulation. During this stage, a woman is accumulating assets, which may include purchasing a home and/or other property. If she is wise, she is also participating in some type of savings plan for retirement. This is done in a variety of ways, including contributing to a retirement plan that has been set up by her employer. Many employers will match your contribution up to a certain point. Some women also have Individual Retirement Accounts (IRAs) that they contribute to.

The goal of the accumulation stage is to allow the value of the assets acquired to increase, so that by the next stage, there will be enough income to live on for the rest of a person's life. The reverse of this is acquiring more debt during what is supposed to be a time of accumulating assets. With that said, some credit purchases can actually be good choices for tax planning and other strategic wealth building purposes. But all too often, I sit down with a woman in her sixties or even seventies who has accumulated very few assets and has huge amounts of debt. This can be disastrous when a person is retired or close to retirement.

Stage #2: Distribution. During this time of life, a person is dependent on distributions from the assets acquired during the accumulation stage. Those who invested in real estate may be enjoying the funds that come from leasing their properties or selling those properties and turning the proceeds into income through other investments. Others may take distributions from the retirement accounts they have been funding over the years. Still others may do a combination of these things. Distribution resources also include Social Security and pensions.

Good tax planning becomes extremely important during the distribution stage. I will discuss certain issues that everyone needs to be aware of regarding taxes during the distribution stage in chapter nine. A lack of good tax planning during this stage can cause a person to have much less to live on, as well as directly affect inheritances.

Stage #3: Preservation. If you are reading this book and are over the age of fifty, chances are you will have at some point in your life been involved with preserving something for the future. For example, if you grew your own produce in a garden, you probably preserved some of it for future use. Did you ever can tomatoes? How nice to be able to go to the pantry and grab a jar of wonderful canned tomatoes to put into your homemade vegetable soup! Or maybe you worked diligently to preserve strawberries for some future enjoyment. Remember popping open the jar top and spreading the preserves on a nice hot biscuit when family came to visit?

Having been raised in the south—Alabama, to be specific—I have always loved fresh garden vegetables. Two of my favorites are purple hull peas and okra. During my twenties, I moved to a northern state and sometimes had difficulty locating these particular vegetables. Being somewhat resourceful, I came up with a plan. I bought an airline ticket, checked myself and two empty suitcases onto a plane and headed south. I bought a bushel each of purple hull peas and okra. I filled the suitcases with these precious commodities and flew them back to my home up north. Immediately after returning, I quickly processed the vegetables and packed them in the freezer. I was oh so happy to have my southern vegetables on hand when I had a craving for them!

The idea behind the preservation stage of finances is the same as what I just described with the tomatoes, strawberry preserves, purple hull peas and okra. The fact that they were preserved to be used at a future time is what the preservation stage is all about. Women must learn how to preserve their assets so that when they need them, they will be available.

Because of poor planning, many women who at one time had plenty of assets find themselves struggling through their retirement years, without enough money to live on. They go to the pantry and find it bare. Their options become very limited. Either they have to go back to work or learn to live on a shoestring budget. Don't let that happen to you!

Some women sacrifice and pinch pennies for years during the accumulation stage to build a fantastic retirement account, at times even accumulating immense wealth. But they mistakenly think that the need for planning stops once they retire. Even those who began retirement with a fantastic portfolio can eventually suffer from inadequate funds if they do not continue to plan during the distribution and preservation stages of their lives.

Stage #4: Transfer. This last stage is the time when assets are passed on to others, either during the benefactor's lifetime or after her passing. Using the proper tax planning tools and legal documents can make all the difference in the world in transferring assets efficiently. The estate planning portion of this book will provide you with several techniques that can have a tremendously positive impact on understanding how to properly transfer assets.

Understanding these four stages and the necessary steps to take during each of them will greatly increase your potential for financial success and security. Just as we have changed and updated the contents of our purses over time, we must also adjust our finances to fit our current needs based on where we are in life.

Empowered For Decision Making

At some point in a woman's life, she will most likely be the one solely responsible for making decisions regarding her finances. Don't get caught off guard!

Knowledge and experience are two key elements for empowering yourself to deal with just about any situation, including making financial decisions. One of the first steps in making a good decision is to understand your options. Next you must evaluate your goals and desires, and third you should be aware of the consequences that accompany your decisions.

The woman who lacks experience in dealing with finances, and has very little knowledge regarding such issues, will find it to be an exceedingly daunting task to manage her financial world.

Today's women are beginning to realize that being informed and experienced in handling finances is no longer optional. They are becoming more and more savvy and confident as they embrace the reality of probable responsibility for their financial well-being.

As you read the information contained in this book, it is my hope that you will begin to feel empowered to make the right decisions to secure your own financial future.

Security System for Your Assets

Why do we install security systems in our houses and automobiles? The answer is simple... to protect our possessions from outside forces that could cause us loss. While we are usually very conscientious in locking the doors to our homes and vehicles, many women haphazardly wander around with little or no protection from the many looming predators that can cause financial devastation for both themselves and their heirs.

Here are some of the leading causes of financial loss that can seriously impact your portfolio during your lifetime and those assets you had planned to pass to your heirs:

1) **Risky Investments.** Whatever your investment strategy is, it should be age appropriate. Timing is everything, including the time of your life. A person who is retired or close to retirement should be much more conservative than a young person who has thirty or forty years left in the workforce.

2) **Loss of Spousal Income.** I'm always amazed when I sit down with a couple whose income will be drastically affected when one of the two passes away; they often have absolutely no plan for spousal income continuation. Many times they will tell me that they can make it without the other's income, but when I bring up such things as inflation and the rising cost of health care, it is like a light bulb going off in their heads for the first time. They immediately realize the colossal negative effect this lack of planning could have on the surviving spouse. Loss of spousal income is one of the leading reasons women struggle financially after their husbands pass away.

3) **Taxes.** I cannot emphasize enough the importance of good tax planning, especially during the distribution and transfer stages. Proper tax planning can drastically increase a person's available cash during their lifetime, as well as make a huge difference in what their heirs will receive at their passing. Some people will exhaust themselves trying to see which bank will pay them 1/4 percent more interest on a CD while they stand by and pay

what is sometimes thousands of dollars in unnecessary taxes. I believe in paying taxes, but only those that are my responsibility.

4) **Lawsuits.** As most people know, we live in a very litigious society. Retirees are sometimes the targets for lawsuits because they are assumed to have accumulated wealth. Protecting yourself from these marauders can be done in a variety of ways. Umbrella policies and certain investment types can shield you from loss due to such unexpected occurrences.

5) **Long-Term Care Cost.** In chapter twelve, I will address the issue of long-term care in more detail. For now, let me just say that such costs can quickly wipe out a lifetime of accumulated assets. Be prepared for some staggering statistics as you move through this book.

6) **Relatives.** Did I say family? Absolutely! And let me be even more specific: grown children. Women love their kids, and when they are in financial trouble, Mom is usually the one who rushes in to make everything "all better." I know this for a fact because I am a mom, and I do not like it when I feel— even if it is just in my own head—that any of my children has a need that is not being met.

While I think it is fine to help your grown children over a little rough spot here and there, or perhaps provide a small short-term loan, I am in complete opposition to what I see many women doing on a constant, on-going basis with their adult children. I have dealt with many women who have practically nothing left to live on because they gave everything away to their children. It makes no sense. Who do they think will have to take care of them when they are elderly and have given all of their funds away: their kids! That is, if their kids are even willing.

Ladies, if you are guilty of this, you have to fix it immediately. The best thing you can do for your children financially is to take care of yourself so that one day they won't have to.

7) **Probate.** Lack of proper planning can result in unnecessary legal fees associated with probate, not to mention the time and aggravation many families experience while going through this process. You can make it much easier for your family to settle your estate if you take the time to do so. Again, this issue will be addressed in more detail later in the book.

Just as most people would not think about leaving home or going to bed at night without locking their doors, we must begin to realize that having that same attitude regarding protecting our assets is imperative. What a shame it would be, after a lifetime of saving and accumulating assets, to allow one or more of the aforementioned predators to creep in and wipe out what is rightly yours and your heirs.

All women deserve to have everything in their "purse" that is needed to be financially secure. With some thoughtful planning and implementation of the **P.U.R.S.E.S.** concept, you can begin your journey now to that desired destination!

CHAPTER SUMMARY

Let's review the acronym P.U.R.S.E.S.:

Purpose Based Planning

Understanding Money Basics

Resources Available

Stages of Life

Empowered for Decision Making

Security System for Your Assets

PURPOSE BASED PLANNING—Having a plan that is based on an intended or desired result to meet the particular needs of the individual.

UNDERSTANDING MONEY BASICS—Having a basic understanding of how money works, how it grows and how to handle it on a day-to-day basis.

RESOURCES AVAILABLE—Being aware of the various investment options and products that are available to you for building your Purpose Based Plan.

STAGES OF LIFE—Understanding the four financial stages of life: accumulation, distribution, preservation and transfer.

EMPOWERED FOR DECISION MAKING—Having the necessary knowledge and experience to make proper decisions regarding your finances and estate plan.

SECURITY SYSTEM FOR YOUR ASSETS—Understanding all of the predators that can cause unnecessary loss to your assets and setting up a system for protection against them.

CHAPTER 2

Statistics That May Shock You

What is the importance of statistics and why is it imperative to analyze them when assembling a financial plan?

Statistics denote probabilities and the likelihood of certain events occurring based on studies, samples and facts. When considering a financial plan, four categories of statistics are critical for providing information necessary for determining goals, needs and plans of action.

Age

Age is the first of the four categories. The age factor can have a profound effect on many parts of a financial plan. For instance, life expectancy is directly related to how many years a person will need income when she no longer receives wages or a salary after retiring from the workforce. With that in mind, let's look at a few statistics regarding age.

- On average, women who reach age sixty-five can expect to live twenty more years. Predictions are that nearly one-third of women who reach age sixty-five can expect to reach age ninety.[1]

Three out of five women over sixty-five cannot afford to cover their basic needs.[15]

- The population age sixty-five and over increased from 35 million in 2000 to 41.4 million in 2011 (an 18 percent increase) and is projected to increase to 79.7 million by 2040.[2]

- Married baby boomer women can expect to outlive their husbands by fifteen to twenty years on the average.[3]

- At age eighty-five, there are twice as many women as men.[4]

- The eighty-five-plus population is projected to increase from 5.7 million in 2011 to 14.1 million in 2040.[5]

Longevity is obviously becoming more of a factor when considering retirement income. If a woman retires at age sixty-five and lives to age ninety (which is very possible, according to the statistics) she will need income for twenty-five years after she has left the workforce! How she will support herself during all those years must be integrated into her overall financial plan.

Another interesting fact involves the number of years a woman will potentially live after her husband passes away. Decreased household income from the loss of a spouse could linger for many years. A good financial plan must take this into consideration to insure a lifetime of financial security. This leads us to our next category of statistics.

Marital Status

- 50 percent of women over 65 are widows.[6]

- 50 percent of first marriages end in divorce.[7]

- In 2009, roughly one in four divorces occurred to persons aged fifty and older. The rate of divorce was 2.5 times higher for those in remarriages versus first marriages.[8]

- The divorce rate for people over age fifty has doubled in the past twenty years.[9]

- In 2013, older men were much more likely to be married than older women, 71 percent of men, 45 percent of women. Widows accounted for 36 percent of all older women. There were over four times as many widows (8.7 million) as widowers (2.3 million).[10]

- The U.S. Census Bureau puts the average age of widowhood at fifty-five.[11]

- Among women aged seventy-five and over, almost half (45 percent) live alone.[12]

- Only 32 percent of women seventy-five-plus years old live with a spouse.[13]

As you will see in the following chapters, marital status directly affects income, taxes and estate planning. A flexible financial plan that can accommodate any marital status is necessary for providing financial security.

Finances

Now let's take a look at some staggering statistics directly related to finances that include such factors as age and marital status.

- 87 percent of the elderly poor are women.[14]

- Three out of five women over sixty-five cannot afford to cover their basic needs.[15]

- A widow is four times more likely—and a single or divorced woman is five times more likely—to live in poverty than a married woman.[16]

- In the first year after a divorce, a woman's standard of living drops an average of 73 percent.[17]

- Most (65 percent) baby boomer women do not have a backup plan if forced into retirement sooner than expected.[18]

- Nearly 4 million of the 10 million-plus women over age fifty-five still are in the workforce. Women make up 46 percent of the total labor force over age sixty-five.[19]

- The average female born between 1948 and 1964 may likely remain in the workforce until at least seventy-four years of age due to inadequate financial savings and pension coverage.[20]

- Retirement benefits are usually one-fourth for women as opposed to men.[21]

- Women are half as likely as men to have an employer-provided pension, and those who do have them get half as much, on average, as men.[22]

- 58 percent of female baby boomers have less than $10,000 in retirement savings.[23]

- Among women thirty-five to fifty-five years old, between one-third and two-thirds will be impoverished by age 70. [24]

- Recently released data from the US Census Bureau reveals that the median amount of debt held by households headed by someone sixty-five or older rose nearly 120 percent between 2000 and 2011, from $12,000 to $26,000. A significant portion of this increase is accounted for by rising mortgage debt because of the collapse of the housing bubble in 2008. [25]

- A 2012 report by The Schwartz Center for Economic Policy found that in 2011, 75 percent of workers between the ages of fifty and sixty-four had less than $30,000 in their retirement accounts. [26]

- A report by the *Wall Street Journal* in 2011 found that the typical American household nearing retirement with a 401(k) savings account had less than one-quarter of what was required to maintain their current standard of living. [27]

- According to the Employee Benefit Research Institute, 43 to 44 percent of boomers may not be able to afford basic living expenses in retirement. [28]

- In 2007, just before the market crisis hit, boomers who were still working expected to retire at an average age of 66.3. In 2011, the average expected age of retirement among working boomers increased to 68.6, and in 2012, the target age climbed to 71.2. [29]

- By 2050, $41 trillion will transfer to the next generation, but much of it will never make it to the intended heirs. [30]

Clearly, these statistics reveal the extreme importance of proactive financial planning! A person who understands this information does not delay; instead, she takes action to position herself for present and future financial security.

In regard to the last statistic, improper tax and estate planning are two of the main reasons why so much of a person's estate will not pass on to her loved ones. However, one of the most common causes for this issue is the rising cost of health care, especially as a person ages.

Health Care

Let's explore a few statistics that will help you understand how devastating the rising cost of health care can be to a person, not only while she is living but also how it can drain her estate and result in a much smaller inheritance for her heirs.

- The Employee Benefit Retirement Institute (EBRI) estimates Medicare pays for only about 60 percent of the cost of health services the typical retiree will need. A couple that is sixty-five today might need nearly $300,000 to cover health costs.[31]

- In 2012, the average annual cost for residing in an assisted living facility was $42,600. The annual rate in a semi-private room in a nursing home averaged $81,030; a private room averaged $90,520 per year.[32]

- Between ages forty and fifty, on average, 8 percent of people have a disability that could require long-term care.[33]

- 70 percent of people turning age sixty-five can expect to use some form of long-term care during their lives.[34]

- Women need care longer (3.7 years) than men (2.2 years), and 20 percent of those needing long-term care will need it for longer than five years.[35]

Many people are under the false assumption that Medicare will cover their long-term care expenses. However, Medicare only pays for long-term care if you require skilled services or rehabilitative care in a nursing home for a maximum of 100 days. The average Medicare covered stay is much shorter (22 days). Medicare does not pay for non-skilled assistance with Activities of Daily Living (bathing, dressing, using the toilet, transferring to or from bed or chair, caring for incontinence, eating).[36]

Based on the statistics above, if a person has $300,000 in retirement savings she was planning to pass on to her heirs but winds up having to pay for a three-year stay in a nursing home, there could potentially be very little left in her estate by the time she passes away.

Hopefully, these statistics will be a motivating factor for women to realize the importance of financial planning. While most women tend to think they will always fall within the most favorable percentage of statistics, the truth is that many will not.

Life holds many uncertainties. No one knows the exact span of their lifetime, how long they may live alone, how long they will be physically able to work or if they will need long-term care at some point. There are no guarantees regarding market conditions, inflation or deflation or the world economy in general.

Many women have a false sense of security. They believe that their current situations will never change. Perhaps they are in a wonderful marriage, have a great job and a large portfolio. They are happy, healthy and content. However, the old cliché holds true, life can turn on a dime. A woman can lose a spouse instantly when her husband has a sudden heart attack, stroke or car accident. Even if death is not the result from these tragedies, lifelong disabilities can occur, causing substantial loss of income and increased expenses that can drain a portfolio.

But one thing is certain: a woman who takes the time to orchestrate a solid financial plan will most certainly find herself far better equipped to handle any circumstance in which she may find herself. On the other hand, a lack of planning can be devastating for any woman. Decide today how important your financial security is to you. The time to begin planning is now, no matter your age, marital status or the size of your portfolio.

CHAPTER SUMMARY

- Women are living longer lives than in the past. Many will reach the age of ninety or beyond.

- Women live an average of seven to ten years longer than men.

- Many women will live a portion of their lives alone due to divorce from, or the death of, their spouse.

- The divorce rate for people fifty and over has doubled in the past twenty years.

- The average age of widowhood is fifty-five.

- A woman's income is normally drastically reduced after losing a spouse.

- Of the elderly living in poverty, three out of four are women.

- Women's retirement benefits are usually one-fourth that of men.

- Only 20 percent of baby boomer women are estimated to be financially secure in their retirement.

- Health costs and long-term care can drain a portfolio.

- An average stay in a nursing home costs between $80,000 and $90,000 annually.

- 70 percent of people turning age sixty-five can expect to use some form of long-term care during their lives.

CHAPTER 3

Reaching Your Goals

In order to be successful in reaching your goals, you must begin with the right attitude. This is true with almost anything in life. Let's begin with two of my favorite quotes from those who have achieved tremendous success. Henry Ford, the founder of the Ford Motor Company, said, "Whether you think you can, or you think you can't—you're right."[1] Lou Holtz, famous Notre Dame football coach, was quoted as saying, "Winners and losers aren't born; they are the products of how they think."[2]

A woman who has the right attitude about reaching her financial goals very likely will achieve them.

Some women have the misconception that financial planning is simply picking a few investments and hoping for the best. This could not be further from the truth. Actually, there are three key components to a financial plan that we will discuss in the chapters to come. But before moving on to those, let's discuss what might be your greatest asset. John Maxwell, author of sixty books and a renowned expert on leadership suggested in his book *The Difference Maker* that our ATTITUDE can be our greatest asset.[3] I absolutely agree.

"Whether you think you can, or you think you can't—you're right."[1]

Over the years, I have encountered women who came from humble beginnings and started with a very small portfolio. Some of these ladies even had limited educational opportunities. But because of their attitudes, they developed into extremely successful women with high net worths. On the other hand, there are thousands of women who begin with large portfolios and because of certain life events, bad spending habits, their own passiveness or no real financial plan, found themselves in critical financial situations and a place of lack.

A woman can almost always put herself into a more favorable financial position, regardless of her age, marital status, education or the size of her portfolio. Here are some interesting facts about millionaires:

1) According to the book *The Millionaire Next Door*, only 20 percent of millionaires inherited their wealth. The other 80 percent earned their cash on their own.

2) Just 17 percent of millionaires or their spouses attended a private elementary or high school.

3) Half of all millionaires are self-employed or own a business. Around 80 percent of millionaires are college graduates. Only 18 percent of millionaires have master's degrees.[4]

MY STORY

I, personally, am a living, breathing example of a woman who was not born into great wealth and had limited resources and educational opportunities. But what I did have was a positive attitude. Please allow me to briefly share my story.

I was born in Sylacauga, Alabama. My mother worked in the town's cotton mill and my father worked in a lumberyard. We did not live in poverty but had a very modest lifestyle. When I was nine years old, my little brother was killed in a terrible accident. Two years later, my father died. My mom, losing her seven-year-old son, and then becoming a widow at an early age, did the best she could to deal with it all, but life was not easy.

I got married at age twenty, and eventually my husband and I brought three amazing sons into the world. Life seemed good and very normal. We were actively involved in ministry and the lives of our children: school functions, Little League games, etc. Holidays were always special in our home, with lots of decorations and hoopla. Our children's many friends made our home the neighborhood hangout, which we loved. Life was a bustling string of basketball games in the driveway, laughter, sit-down dinners at home, and fun church activities and youth group trips.

My husband and I were so blessed to have three such wonderful sons, each one bringing so much joy to our sweet family. Then the unthinkable happened. Before I knew it, my wonderful life of bliss was turned upside down. Without going into the many details that led up to this disaster, let me just say that I found myself involved in a divorce that would have been unimaginable to me in the years before.

There I was, with no husband and no job. I had two sons in college at that time and my youngest was a senior in high school. Our home eventually went into foreclosure and was sold on the courthouse steps. Fortunately, before we lost our home, I was able to establish housing for myself and my sons in rental properties.

I had always assisted my husband in whatever he was involved in but had done very little to establish myself in any particular career. I did have a few accomplishments under my belt, including writing and producing televised children's musicals and helping to start a Christian school and two childcare centers that are still operational today and highly successful. However, I had moved on from all of those programs, and any revenue I had received for my involvement with them was in the past.

Even though I had always been creative, energetic and a positive thinker, I felt that my options for employment were limited. Most jobs that paid a good salary required either more experience or a higher level of education than I possessed.

I had a decision to make. I could turn my hurt and grief from my divorce into bitterness and live out the rest of my days complaining about the injustices done to me, or I could figure out a way to move forward, rise above the devastating circumstances and reclaim a life of hope and happiness. I decided on the latter.

My ex-husband had spent our last few years together working as a financial adviser. Even though I was not a licensed adviser, I was familiar with the business from a marketing perspective. I decided to pursue a career in financial planning. I began attending the required classes and eventually passed all the tests needed for licensing.

The first job I took as a licensed adviser involved cold calling business owners. The company I worked for provided fee-based planning in the business owner market. If you have ever done any type of cold calling, you know the difficulty of that task. If not, believe me, it is one of the hardest in the world! Many of the advisers in the company had a very short career there. They couldn't take the constant rejection.

However, I pushed on and stuck it out long enough to establish myself in the industry. I knew I had to be successful in this position if I were ever going to move to the next level. Eventually, I was hired by a company for which I began making a substantial income. After several years of working in the financial services industry, I ventured out and began my own businesses. I now own three very successful companies: one financial planning company and two marketing companies.

Even though it probably took you less than five minutes to read the last few paragraphs, it took years of hard work, determination, tenacity and fortitude for me to move from a place of emotional and financial devastation to one of financial freedom and security. I cannot even begin to count the number of times I listened to a Les Brown CD entitled, *It's Not Over Until I Win*. I repeated to myself over and over his inspiring words: "No matter how hard it is or how hard it gets, I'm going to make it."

Through my own experience, I have found another famous quote from Lou Holtz to be true: "Life is ten percent what happens to you and ninety percent how you respond to it."[5] I believe any woman can reach her goals no matter what her current situation, but it does takes effort and a plan. Most of us have heard the old cliché, Successful people are willing to do what unsuccessful people are not. That is another statement I believe is true.

LIFE CHANGING D WORDS

I would like to share with you eight D words that will help lead you to your goals regardless of where you are in life and what circumstances may be surrounding you:

DREAM. Don't hold back; dream big. If you can believe it, you can achieve it! Reconnect to the dreams you once had. Some women have been so caught up in the busyness of life that they have forgotten what their preferences are. Visualize what reaching your financial goals could mean to your life. The dream will keep you going on days when you feel you are losing steam. Some people make dream books to help them stay focused. They fill a scrapbook or photo album with pictures or magazine clippings of all the things they dream about. Dream books can consist of just about anything. Make your dream book unique to what makes you feel happy and secure.

DESTINATION. You must decide where you want to go. That will define your goals. You must determine your point A (your starting point), declare your point B (where you want to end up) and then decide how you will get there.

DECISION. Many times we are only a few decisions away from realizing our dreams. Reaching a goal will require decision making, something that many women are not comfortable with. If you struggle with making decisions, you must change that today. You will need to decide when to turn right, when to turn left, when to stand still and when to move forward.

DETOX. This means getting rid of the toxins that can keep you from reaching your goals. Here are a few of the poisons that need to be dealt with. The first one is worry. Did you know that 80 percent of the things we worry about never happen? Worry will drain you of your energy and take your focus away from reaching your goals. Next are the attitude toxins, such as anger, bitterness and resentment. Again, these will zap your energy and create diversions that will take you off course. Fear is also poisonous. Many women are paralyzed by fear, leaving them frozen and never able to move toward their goals. Then there are the toxic naysayers who constantly discourage you and tell you why you can't do something or why your idea will never work. Get away from these negative people and surround yourself with positive, successful ones instead.

The list of toxins goes on. These can include bad spending habits that can cripple your chances of reaching your goals. Bad relationships can also be a constant distraction. And then there is the poison of excuses. Too many times, we make excuses for ourselves: not enough education, too young, too old, too busy, etc. Excuses will keep you on a treadmill to nowhere. Detox today! Get rid of all of the things in your life that are holding you back.

DO LIST. Begin to jot down the things you must do to reach your goals. As you move through the pages of this book, there will be instructions and checklists to help you write your do list.

DISCIPLINE. Once you begin the journey to reach your goals, there will be times you must maintain strict discipline. Distractions can steal your focus. Bad habits, like overspending and procrastination, will try to creep in. Without discipline, achieving your goals will be virtually impossible.

DETERMINATION. Remember, your attitude is critical. You must learn to turn obstacles into opportunities. Don't quit. Remember Les Brown's famous speech that I referenced earlier: "It's Not Over Until I Win." Remind yourself that no matter how hard it is, or how hard it gets, you're going to make it. That is the type of tenacity required to reach a goal. Be determined to keep moving and no matter what direction you take, make sure it is forward!

DEADLINE. A goal without a deadline is just a dream. Setting deadlines will keep you moving and on pace to reach your destination. Without a deadline, a goal will almost never become a reality.

BASIC FINANCIAL GOALS FOR WOMEN

I believe there are five goals every woman should strive for: **FINANCIAL SUCCESS, FINANCIAL FREEDOM, FINANCIAL RESONSIBILITY, FINANCIAL INDEPENDENCE and FINANCIAL SECURITY**. Each woman will need to interpret these goals according to her own desires, dreams and needs. Let me take a moment to define in simple terms what each of these actually means.

FINANCIAL SUCCESS. The opposite of success is failure. We want to avoid financial failure at all cost (no pun intended). Failure also means insufficiency. Since failure is the opposite of success, insufficiency is the opposite of sufficiency. Thus, in my opinion, financial success is having sufficient funds to fulfill our basic needs and achieve all of our financial goals. Financial success can even catapult us toward fulfilling desires that go beyond necessity, including such things as travel, gifting and other items we won't die without but would be really nice to be able to enjoy.

FINANCIAL FREEDOM. What do you want to be free from regarding your finances? How about free from stress and worry? That, in and of itself, is tremendous freedom! How nice it would be to never spend another sleepless night worrying about your finances, being able to spend money traveling or shopping without having to live with the regret of spending money you really don't have. If your girlfriends, church or community invite you to participate in a trip, how wonderful to be in a position to say yes instead of having to decline because of a lack of funds. You get the idea; financial freedom is simply being free to do the things you want to do without worry or stress regarding money. Sounds good, right?

FINANCIAL RESPONSIBILITY. This is taking your financial future into your own hands. Does it mean not having a financial professional to help guide you? No, it simply means that you stop relying on someone else to totally take care of your finances without any involvement or oversight on your part.

Begin taking responsibility today. If you are married and know nothing about your financial situation, let your spouse know how important it is for you to become informed. Be adamant and do not take no for an answer. Remember, you have every right to know what is going on with your finances. If you are working with an unproductive adviser and the only person who is making money with your portfolio is him/her, fire that person and find someone you can trust who has your best interests at heart. Some financial professionals treat women like little children. I have women tell me that when they call their financial adviser to discuss their concerns over declines, the adviser's response is simply, "Don't worry your pretty little head; everything will be all right." How condescending! No woman should put up with that, even when the adviser's intentions are good. You deserve more than just a pat on the head when you are trying to retrieve information regarding something of such huge importance as your finances.

FINANCIAL INDEPENDENCE. Become a woman who does not have to rely on others for her financial stability and security. Position yourself so that no matter what happens, you will be able to care for yourself financially.

After being divorced for several years, I was blessed to find an amazing man whom I eventually married. But, you should know, my husband and I are both financially independent of each other. Does this mean we never discuss our financial decisions together? Of course not! We talk about pretty much everything, including all major financial decisions. But if something happened to my husband—death, divorce or disability—I still would be financially secure. If something happened to me, my husband would also be fine financially.

In addition to being financially independent from our spouses, we should also quit relying so heavily on other sources I will discuss in the next chapter. We all hope life will go smoothly and nothing will upset the apple cart, but in reality, that rarely happens. If you are financially independent, these episodes will have a minimal effect on your financial future.

FINANCIAL SECURITY. This should be every woman's ultimate goal. Women love feeling secure; it's just the way we are made. There are few things more upsetting than feeling we are exposed and vulnerable, especially financially. We must take whatever steps necessary to achieve that security.

A woman who is willing to take the time and exert the energy to put together a well-thought-out Purpose Based Plan will achieve each of these five goals and find herself in a healthy, secure financial position.

CHAPTER SUMMARY

Your attitude can be your greatest asset.

Anyone can be successful, but it takes effort and a plan.

Eight D words that can help your reach your goals:

- **Dream.** Don't hold back. If you can believe it, you can achieve it!

- **Destination.** You must decide where you want to go.

- **Decision.** Many times you are only a few decisions away from realizing your dreams.

- **Detox.** Rid yourself of the toxins that can keep you from reaching your goals.

- **Do List.** Write down the things you must do to reach your goals.

- **Discipline.** Maintain strict discipline and avoid distractions that can steal your focus.

- **Determination.** Don't quit! Keep moving forward!

- **Deadline.** A goal without a deadline is just a dream.

Five goals for a woman's financial plan:

- **Financial Success.** Having sufficient funds to achieve all of her financial goals and needs.

- **Financial Freedom**. Being free to function financially without worry or stress.

- **Financial Responsibility**. Taking responsibility for your own financial wellness.

- **Financial Independence**. Not having to rely on others for your financial stability and security.

- **Financial Security**. Achieving a place of financial certainty that eliminates or at least minimizes exposure and vulnerability.

CHAPTER 4

Money Myths

Mastering the ability to secure your financial future involves understanding what is real versus what is false regarding money. Over the years, women have developed mindsets about finances that are based on inaccurate information and misguided teaching. This misinformation has led them to make poor financial decisions or no decisions at all. A series of problems and mistakes can occur when women are poorly equipped or possess the wrong attitude toward money and finances.

To obtain financial success and lasting security, it may be necessary to disabuse yourself of some myths in which women have been tangled up for many years. Some of these misconceptions and beliefs have been handed down from past generations and, sadly, even taught in some religious arenas. No wonder women have struggled to interpret their roles when it comes to handling money.

As we take a look at ten of those myths, ask yourself if any of them have ever held you hostage, preventing you from taking necessary steps to be better informed about financial issues.

A man is not a financial plan.

Myth #1. I Would Be Showing Disrespect to My Husband If I Tried to Be More Involved in Our Finances.

Having involvement in the family finances has absolutely nothing to do with respect. A woman can respect her husband in many ways and still be as involved in the finances as he is. Some men try to shelter their wives from the "burden" of having to deal with finances. While this is admirable, it is not wise. One never knows when a wife will be left to make financial decisions on her own. If a man is *purposely* keeping his wife in the dark about their finances, that usually is about one of two things: either he is hiding something or it makes him feel powerful and builds his ego. A woman not only has the right but the responsibility to be informed about her family's finances.

A woman should also understand that she has the right to make financial decisions. While my husband and I make almost every major financial decision together, there are times when I make a decision about one of my businesses alone. Or I may decide to spend money on a trip or purchase a clothing item or something for our home without discussing it at length with my husband. But I never do that in a disregarding or disrespectful way. My husband knows full well that I respect his position in our home and highly value his opinion.

Myth #2. I Don't Have to Concern Myself With Money Issues Because I Have a Man to Rely On.

Can I let you in on a little secret? A MAN IS NOT A FINANCIAL PLAN. When I am holding a P.U.R.S.E.S. workshop, I always have the women repeat that phrase after me. While they get a big kick out of it, and we laugh at the words, there are still women who absolutely believe that their financial plan is a man, even if they refuse to admit it to themselves or others.

At times, I have asked women what they would do financially if their husband passed away first. Believe it or not, I have actually received answers back that go something like: "Oh, I would just find myself another man." Some women are in complete denial and won't even face the fact that it is possible they could be left on their own. As we discussed in chapter 3, there are many things that can happen to a man that would leave a woman to fend for herself, including death, divorce and disability.

Prince Charming Isn't Coming by Barbara Stanny is a wonderful book. Barbara is the daughter of one of the founders of H & R Block. She grew up depending first on her father and later her husband to manage her money, until a devastating crisis served as a dramatic wake-up call for her.

As you read in the last chapter, I experienced a completely unexpected divorce after twenty-four years of marriage that threw my financial world into chaos. I was totally unprepared to handle this upheaval, and I faced a long, hard road to recovery. Perhaps that is why I am so passionate about women being responsible for securing their own financial futures. As I mentioned earlier, I have remarried to a wonderful man and our finances are stable and secure. But I did not marry him to be my financial security. By the time we met, I had already established my own companies and was making a great living for myself. If something ever happened to him, including death, divorce or disability, I would certainly be distraught emotionally, but my financial world would remain stable and secure.

Myth #3. I Don't Have to Concern Myself With Money Issues Because I Plan to Inherit Plenty From My Family.

Many wealthy people have passed away leaving very little to their heirs. There are a number of reasons for this. First, some supposed heirs are shocked to discover that their parent(s) intentionally left very little, if any, of their assets to them in their wills. Being involved with estate planning, I can certainly attest to this fact. When some of my clients inform me of the desired beneficiaries of their accounts, it is not uncommon for them to bypass their own children or leave only a small portion to them. What I often hear regarding their reasoning for this is that either they feel their children are doing quite well themselves and don't really need the money, or they just want to leave their estate to other places, such as charities.

Secondly, many people unintentionally disinherit their heirs because of poor, or no, estate planning. What assets they leave behind are used up to pay taxes, unpaid debts, legal fees, etc.

Another common cause for expected inheritances to never materialize is a catastrophic event that wipes out large amounts of assets in the last years of a person's life, such as long-term care. And even if an inheritance is probable at some point, some parents wind up living well into their nineties or beyond. By the time a child receives that inheritance, they are already well into retirement themselves.

Depending on an inheritance to fund your retirement can be somewhat shaky thinking, to say the least. I strongly suggest letting the inheritance be a bonus, not your financial plan.

Myth #4. I Am Secure at the Company I Work For.

Several years ago, I received a call from a lady who sounded panic-stricken. She began to tell me about the events that had taken place only a few hours earlier. For privacy's sake, I will call her Stacie. After climbing the corporate ladder, Stacie landed a high-paying position that gave her authority over a great many employees, as well as being responsible for key operations of the company.

Stacie reported to work one day as usual only to be notified that she no longer had a position with the company. She was told that a decision had been made to restructure, which meant that her position was being eliminated. The only thing they could offer her was a cardboard box in which to pack her personal items. Without any prior warning or notice, her job was gone, just like that. Stacie never expected to lose her job at the company for which she had been working for years.

According to the US Department of Labor, the number of unemployed persons in June 2009 was 14.7 million, with the unemployment rate at 9.5 percent. Since the start of the recession that began in December 2007, the number of unemployed persons increased by 7.2 million, and the unemployment rate rose by 4.6 percentage points. Let these statistics always be a reminder of what can happen to jobs during an economic crisis.

This loss of jobs affected people of all ages. I recently had a lady who held an executive position with a major company call my office for an appointment. She wanted to discuss her recent loss of employment. This sweet lady, already in her sixties, was making plans to move from her home of many years to a small, modest apartment as a result of inadequate savings and job loss. I felt so bad for her, but there was very little advice I could give her. With the unemployment rate what it was, and given her age, her options were extremely limited.

Every woman who is still in the workforce needs to have adequate savings, especially in light of what we experienced during the last recession. Don't leave yourself without options!

Myth #5. I Can Depend on the Government to Take Care of Me.

I barely know how to comment on this one. With the worst economic devastation since the Great Depression and the enormous debt faced by our federal government, please do not rely on this source for the security of your financial future. While I am trusting that Social Security benefits will last for those who are already receiving them, I can tell you that as a fifty-seven-year-old woman, I am definitely not basing my future income on a check from the government. Considering what I have paid into this program over the years, I would be delighted to receive some compensation from it, but if I do, I will look at it as a bonus and be grateful.

At the writing of this book, the national debt was over $17 trillion. This is what that looks like in figures: $17,000,000,000,000. This translates into each citizen owing over $55,000, or $151,000 per tax payer.[1] Even though we may never be called upon individually to pay those amounts, I have included the numbers to provide an example of why we should not be reliant upon the government for our financial security.

A trillion $10 bills end to end would wrap around the globe 380 times. This would still not be nearly enough to pay off the national debt.[2]

According to Randomhistory.com on the subject of debt crisis, the US government borrows approximately $5 billion every business day.[3]

Considering these staggering facts, do you really feel like depending on the government should be your sole plan for your financial future?

Myth # 6. Women Aren't Supposed to Understand Money Matters.

There is nothing spiritual, sexy, feminine or cute about being misinformed about money. As a matter of fact, most men are intrigued by women who are financially savvy. I have even heard men say that they think a woman who is financially astute is sexy. Don't ever play dumb about money for the sake of stoking a man's ego. This really won't serve you well at all.

Some women really are convinced that men are smarter when it comes to money. This is a delusion that has held a grip on women for years. There is absolutely no foundation on which to base this. Think about the many accomplishments of brilliant women such as astronauts, scientists, doctors, philosophers, physicists… the list goes on and on. Are we supposed to believe that on the subject of money and finances, women just naturally possess a mental block? Think about how ridiculous that notion is.

Women must move past these unfounded beliefs and begin to realize the importance of being informed and educated regarding money matters.

Myth #7. The More Money a Person Has, the More Materialistic They Are.

Materialism is about attitudes, not assets. There are women who have very little but are extremely materialistic. They are always preoccupied with acquiring stuff. These women have a constant thirst for more things. Often they are the very ones who wind up facing retirement with heavy debt and very few assets. It seems ironic, but it is true.

There are other women who have many assets but do not have an attitude of materialism. Through a lifetime of saving for the future, making wise financial decisions and smart investment choices and, sometimes, just being blessed in general, they have managed to acquire assets or even great wealth, but still they remain untainted by a materialistic attitude.

Being poor, rich or somewhere in between does not make you materialistic. That comes from a mindset and is determined by your own attitude toward possessions.

Myth #8. Money Causes a Person To Be Proud.

Again, pride is an attitude of the heart. Many wealthy people are actually quite humble, while some poor people possess very prideful hearts. Women with very little means can be uppity and snooty, while women who possess great wealth may be unpretentious and kind.

Don't judge a person's heart by their possessions. You will know a person who is full of pride by her behavior, not by what she is wearing, where she lives, what kind of car she drives or even the brand of purse she carries!

Myth #9. Rich People are Greedy.

You can be poor as dirt and still be greedy. Just as materialism and pride are attitudes of the heart, so is greed. It really has nothing to do with financial status. Are there wealthy people who are greedy? Absolutely! But some of the wealthiest people in the world are also some of the most generous.

Look around at many entrepreneurs, sports figures and celebrities. The tremendous contributions made by these wealthy individuals certainly do not denote an attitude of greed. Quite the contrary, many times their generosity literally changes the lives of the underprivileged and brings the light of hope into a bad situation.

Myth #10. The Bible Says Money Is the Root of Evil.

Absolutely untrue! The Bible says, "The *love* of money is the root of all kinds of evil."[4] There's the attitude factor again. Things, money, possessions in and of themselves are not evil. How we feel about them is what determines whether there is any evil involved.

If making money and possessing things are the priorities of our lives and cause us to ignore our family, responsibilities and the needs of others, then chances are our attitude regarding money is wrong. But the fact that a person has wealth definitely does not make her evil.

Now is the time for moving past these unfounded and somewhat ridiculous myths. Do not allow old mindsets and misinformation to guide you. The result of doing so will most likely deter you from reaching your potential as an informed and confident financial decision maker.

CHAPTER SUMMARY

- There is no disrespect to your husband in your being informed about the family finances. You not only have the right but you have a responsibility to do so.

- A MAN IS NOT A FINANCIAL PLAN. Need I say more?

- Many people will never receive the inheritance they are expecting or relying on.

- There really is no such thing as job security.

- The government is not in a position to provide financial security for all citizens. Make sure you have an alternate plan for taking care of yourself.

- Being ignorant about finances does nothing to make a woman more charming. Women can be just as competent as men regarding financial decision making.

- Having money does not mean a person is materialistic.

- Pride is an attitude of the heart and can come in many forms. Money does not necessarily cause a person to be prideful.

- Greed can be present in both the wealthy and the poor, just as generosity and charity can exude from both.

- Money does not make a person evil; it is a person's attitude about money that matters.

CHAPTER 5

Creating A Money Garden

Money does not grow on trees. I'm sure you've heard that old cliché many times and, quite possibly, have repeated it to your children to prove a point: money doesn't come easily. But while it does not grow on trees, nor does it come easily, it can *grow* if you know how to create a money garden. And for any type of garden—vegetable, herb or flower—there is a process that must be followed to produce a good crop. The same principles hold true for the money garden. Over time, with effort and care, a money garden can produce an abundance of financial security.

SEVEN PRINCIPLES FOR GROWING A SUCCESSFUL GARDEN

1) **PLOW.** This is a time of preparation: maybe pursuing a college education, researching a business opportunity, etc. This is the time to consider your gifts, talents and what you enjoy doing.

2) **PLANT.** Once you choose your path for making money, you begin to sow seeds. These consist of time, labor, energy and money.

Money is not evil; money is good.
The position you give it in your
life is what matters.

3) **PRUNE.** As time goes by, you decide what is working in your garden and what no longer needs to be there. Rid yourself of anything that may be holding you back from reaching your goals. Remember the toxins that were discussed in chapter 3? These can become weeds in your garden. If not removed, those toxins will be like weeds that take over, choking the life out of your dreams and goals.

4) **PRODUCE.** As you work toward your goals, you begin to produce a garden of financial security. Income, assets and retirement savings begin to grow in the money garden.

5) **PICK.** This is harvest time. You are at the place for enjoying the fruit of your labor. If you have taken good care of your garden, there will be an abundance for you to enjoy.

6) **PRESERVE.** Not only will you need assets today, but you must plan for tomorrow. Your cupboards must never be empty! You must insure that you will have enough to last a lifetime.

7) **PASS.** The last phase of a garden is after you have preserved all that is needed for yourself; you will probably want to pass the rest to others.

Wouldn't you love to have a money garden that flourishes? Most everyone would! The seven P principles seem relatively simple, right? However, putting them into action and actually growing that garden takes effort on your part. From the groundbreaking process of plowing to the harvesting phase and beyond, we must be attentive and actively involved in the process.

Every woman can have a green thumb when it comes to growing a money garden. But without a proper prospective on money and an understanding of the gardening process, a woman will fail and find herself lacking the financial security she was hoping for.

FREEDOM

We must begin to understand that financial success is not just a number in our checkbook or at the end of a brokerage statement. Money affects practically every part of our lives. You have probably heard another old cliché: money cannot buy happiness. While I tend to agree with that to a point, I believe that money can provide many things that do make a person happy, or at least improves their quality of life.

One of the things that money certainly does provide is *freedom*. Let's review some various freedoms money can offer.

- **Freedom from stress**. How often have you been stressed out, worried about your financial situation? Not having enough money to meet a budget or purchase the things you need can put an enormous amount of stress on a person or a family. Financial stress is one of the leading causes of divorce. Stress can also have a very negative impact on your health.

- **Freedom from hectic lifestyles and undesirable chores.** People with plenty of money do not have to fill their calendars with things they may not enjoy doing, such as cleaning house, lawn maintenance, running errands, laundry, washing automobiles, etc. They simply hire people to do those tasks for them. If you are a person who enjoys working in your yard, it is fine to keep this on your personal to-do list, but it is nice for chores to be optional rather than a burden that may keep you from doing other things you like more. Sometimes women convince themselves that they enjoy the chores simply because they don't see another alternative.

- **Freedom to travel.** Most people love to travel; however, many people don't travel simply because they cannot afford to. Of course, not all vacations and trips need to be costly. But as someone who has traveled to many places all over the world, there is no doubt that flights, nice hotels, cruises, etc., can certainly take a toll on the old pocketbook.

- **Freedom to spend more time with those you love**. Once you have the money to hire someone to handle the tasks you don't want to do yourself, you will find much more time can be spent with your family and friends. Ask yourself: would you rather spend time mopping floors or doing more enjoyable things such as having lunch with friends, taking your daughter shopping or spending time on the playground with your grandchildren?

- **Freedom to do the things you want to do**. Many people get up every morning and spend the entire day without doing one thing they really like to do. If you have money, you have the freedom to choose what you want to do with your day. Maybe you would love to go to the gym more, read a book, ride a bike or work on a craft.

- **Freedom to buy what you want when you want it**. I realize that at first this comes off as sounding a bit materialistic, but remember what I said back in chapter 4 about materialism. There is nothing wrong with being able to purchase what you want if you can afford it.

Let me reiterate, many women have the wrong perception of what money can actually do for a person. While the cash itself may not do anything to bring you happiness, the freedom it brings can most certainly lessen your stress and greatly enhance your quality of life.

Money is not evil; money is good. The position you give it in your life is what matters. If you forsake your loved ones and your health due to chasing after the almighty dollar and become a workaholic, then money is probably not in its proper place in your life. However, if you can get a healthy prospective on money, put together a plan that will build your portfolio without other areas of your life suffering, the end result will most likely be a newfound freedom and an enhanced quality of life for you and those you love.

Over the years, as my businesses grew and were successful, I learned a lot about money and how it could be used to make my life better. In addition, the money I earned has afforded me the ability to help others. I have had the opportunity to travel to many wonderful and exciting destinations around the world, at times bringing along friends or family. I have a lovely home where my family and friends gather, making cherished memories. Money has allowed me to help others in need, support nonprofit organizations and employ people.

In short, money has allowed me the freedom to go where I want to go, buy what I want to buy, live where I want to live and bless others all along the way. Is there really any evil in that? Absolutely not!

One thing to remember is that freedom is not free. I did not wake up one day and find myself lying in a bed of money. I never won the lottery or received an inheritance. As I've mentioned, my parents were certainly not wealthy. The recipe for any success I may have achieved is the same as that of many others who are financially free: hard work, determination, making the most of every opportunity and constantly trying to help others along my journey.

Sometimes people look at the wealthy and think, *Oh, how lucky they are.* Most times, luck has very little to do with it, and it certainly didn't in my case. In many card and board games, luck is about 90 percent responsible for determining the winner. Other games require much more strategic moves, such as thinking ahead, plotting out a course of action and overcoming challenges from opponents. Wow, that sounds a lot like financial planning!

Some people struggle with the thought of having money. It's not that they don't want it; it is just that they are not willing to put forth the effort to make it. And that is fine, if that is their choice. But many times that choice results in them working even harder to try to handle all of their tasks and deal with the stresses of not having enough money.

I am certainly not advocating that everyone must be rich to be happy, not at all. But many people are just a few decisions away from turning their bad financial situation into one that brings tremendous freedom to their life. In the next chapter, we will explore many mistakes women make regarding finances. Avoiding these mistakes is paramount to financial success. But before we go there, let's take a few moments to consider ways of making money and the steps necessary to hanging on to it.

MAKING MONEY

The opportunities and resources that are available today for making money are limitless. While many women still work in the corporate world, there are more and more turning to business ownership or becoming savvy investors. The Internet has changed the face of how a person can make money. Multitudes of people are making a great living without ever walking out their front door.

Robert Kiyosaki's very popular book, *Rich Dad's Cashflow Quadrant: Rich Dad's Guide to Financial Freedom,* described four areas where people make money: employee, self-employed, business owner and investor.[1] All of these areas help make the world go round. You will have to decide which one is the better fit for you.

An *employee* works for another person or company. Someone else determines their job responsibilities and required hours. An employee is expected to complete tasks that fall within their job description (and sometimes outside of it as well). This is done in exchange for consistent wages or a salary.

Normally, an employee does not have to worry about the overhead of the business or the overall business plan. Nor does an employee spend much time thinking about their job once their workday is over. These are benefits to being an employee. However, there are also restrictions. Many employees have very little freedom to decide how many days they would like to take off or how many hours each day they want to work. Salary heights that can be reached are also often restricted.

Self-employed people have almost the exact opposite freedoms and restrictions as employees. While they have much flexibility in determining their hours, vacation time and salary potential, those who are self-employed must carry the weight of any overhead they may have, as well as do the business planning. The responsibility of making sure they are making money is a very different process from that of an employee, who receives a guaranteed weekly or monthly paycheck.

Next is the *business owner.* The United States was built by those brave souls who believed in their ideas enough to take on enormous risks, work extremely hard and maintain discipline, focus and determination. The end result: a business.

Business owners provide employment for others, which means that not only are they responsible for their own paycheck but that of others as well, who are depending on the continued success of the business.

Half of all millionaires are self-employed or own a business.[2] While these two options for earning money may be harder in one way, they could pay off in the long run. Only you can decide if being self-employed or a business owner is right for you. Obviously, many people who are self-employed also own a business.

Another fabulous way of making money is through *investing*. An investment can be made through your time, your money or a combination of the two. Both time and money are of considerable value. One place where people fail miserably while trying to build wealth is in not placing the correct value on their time.

Years ago, when I began my career as a financial adviser, one of my first mentors said to me, "Bobbie, you are a $150-an-hour person doing $10-an-hour work." That statement never left me. As time progressed, I learned the value of paying someone to carry out many tasks for me, which freed me up to handle the things I was uniquely qualified for. Because I was a perfectionist and somewhat of a control freak, it wasn't easy for me to make that transition. But over time, I realized that there were a great many people who could handle certain things almost as well as I did, the same as I did, or far better than I did. I quickly learned to surround myself with people who could use their gifts, talents and abilities to help me reach my goals. At the same time, those people were being given employment and the opportunity to reach their own goals.

The tasks I assigned to others fell into three categories: the ones I didn't have time to do, the ones I didn't want to do and the ones I was less qualified to do. You will notice that I didn't say anything about things I was not willing to do. *Not wanting to do something* and *not being willing to do something* are very different things.

Since I was a teenager, I have been willing to do almost any task that needed to be done. I have made money babysitting, cleaning other people's homes, cleaning commercial buildings, being a cashier and a receptionist, working in a garment factory, cold calling, etc. At one time I held a job that required me to drive an enormous number of miles—up to 1,000 some weeks! The list goes on and on. And guess what? If my life required that I fill one of those positions again, I would definitely be willing to do so. None of those jobs are beneath me. I have respect for all workers. I have always tried to make the best of any situation in which I worked and found joy in each of the positions I held along the way.

With that being said, however, even though a person may be willing to do a certain task, it doesn't necessarily mean it is the wisest thing for them to do. That will depend on where you are in life. For those who are just starting out in the workforce or, perhaps, still in college or graduate school, taking a position that may not be your dream job can make perfect sense.

Some women with small children may prefer to babysit other people's children rather than leave their own home each day to go to a job. Based on Salary.com's 13th Annual Mom Salary Survey, if a stay-at-home mom was paid for all of the hours she worked at home and the tasks she performed, her annual salary would be $113,568. This is based on an annual salary of $38,126 which includes forty regular and fifty-six overtime hours per week. [3] If a woman has a job outside of the home, but most of what she earns is eaten away by taxes, childcare, etc., it could make more sense for her to delay seeking employment.

Each woman has to decide what is best for her situation. Basically, any job that helps you meet your needs and goals is a good choice.

However, every woman owes it to herself to consider all of her options. If hiring other people to do certain tasks will help you reach your goals faster, why not do so? Not only do I employ people to fill positions in my companies, I also pay someone to clean my house, wash my car and maintain my property.

This may not be making sense to you yet. You may still be thinking, *If I am spending all of this money to pay others, how does that help me make money?* Let's look at one example: If you have the talent and opportunity to make $50 per hour, but you are not free to do so because you have too many other things that need to be done, such as house cleaning, laundry, etc., wouldn't it make sense to pay someone $10 or $20 per hour to handle those chores for you? If you made $50 per hour, and you just worked part time—let's say twenty hours per week—that amounts to $1,000 per week. If you hired someone to take care of your home, or whatever other tasks needed to be done, and you paid them $15 per hour, your outgo would be $300 per week if they worked the same twenty hours. Let's do the math: $1,000 – $300 = $700. This leaves you $700 per week to spend on the things that you love: maybe things for yourself, your family or your favorite charity. Or what about investing that $700 back into your money garden and growing it for an even greater return?

Get ready for another old cliché: work smarter, not harder. Many people make life much harder on themselves than necessary by not following that principle. They are living far below their potential simply due to a wrong way of thinking.

As I mentioned earlier, there is nothing wrong with taking care of your own chores. Just make sure they are the ones that you enjoy. Be careful not to fall in the world of complacency, in which you will fail to live life to its fullest. We all have only one life. Stop and allow yourself to think about your goals and dreams. Then go for them. Decide what you can do on your own and what tasks you need to hire others to accomplish. You may decide to begin by paying someone else to drive your children to soccer practice or do your grocery shopping for you. If delegating those tasks to someone else positions you to reach your goals faster, why wouldn't you consider that course of action?

Now that you understand that the way you invest your time is a very critical decision, you will see that the same holds true for how you invest your money. As I said in chapter 1, the R in P.U.R.S.E.S. stands for Resources. There are multitudes of investments to choose from. Some people invest in real estate; others prefer having a brokerage account with a variety of investments such as stocks, bonds and mutual funds. Still others invest in a business of their own. Investing is something that should be taken very seriously and done after careful consideration of all your options, your risk tolerance and how the investments will help you reach your goals.

Your time horizon also plays a very important part in your investment decision making. Do you need a short-term investment or something that is more long-term? Another words, when will you need the money?

Tax planning, which we will explore in detail in chapter 9, will also be very important as you pick your investments. Would you rather pay taxes as you go or pay them in the future? Vehicles that allow you to delay paying taxes on earnings are considered to be tax-deferred. This is the case with plans such as a 401k, 403b, SEP or IRA.

For some, paying taxes in the future makes more sense, especially those who are currently in a high income-tax bracket. Delaying could result in a tax savings. On the other hand, as you get older, you may not have the write offs you have right now, such as mortgage interest. All of these things need to be considered as you design your financial plan.

SAVING FOR THE FUTURE

As you build your portfolio, one thing is for sure: you must put a portion of your earnings aside for retirement. If you are already retired, making extremely wise investment choices and protecting those investments is imperative. Let's explore some ways to save money for retirement, as well as dealing with investments once you are no longer in the workforce.

Retirement vehicles for employees may consist of company pensions, which are becoming less popular, or programs such as 401ks, 403bs or deferred compensation. Some companies offer both: a pension and another vehicle such as a 401k. There are many companies that will contribute to a plan for you and/or match what you contribute yourself. In my opinion, if a company is willing to match your investment, that is automatically a 100 percent return. Anytime someone asks me about contributing to an employer plan that offers a match, I usually tell them to max out whatever the match is. For instance, if an employer will match up to 5 percent of a person's salary, it is usually wise for the employee to contribute at least that 5 percent toward the plan.

If you are self-employed, there are many plans available for tax-deferred savings, such as a SEP or Keogh. Plans vary as far as maximum contribution allowed and who else must be included in the plan if you have employees. Your financial adviser or CPA can help instruct you on which plan might be best for you.

Many people contribute to Traditional or Roth IRAs. Again, there are restrictions on annual contributions.

No matter which vehicle(s) you choose to invest in, saving for retirement is essential for establishing financial security when you are no longer in the workforce. As I have said, contributing to retirement accounts while you are working offers a wonderful benefit in that it can reduce your tax liability while you are in a higher income-tax bracket. You pay lower taxes now and receive an additional benefit once you retire: money to live on.

There are many ways to save for retirement. The goal is to have income once you are no longer in the workforce.

We will discuss how savings in a qualified account such as a 401K or SEP can be used for retirement income in chapter 8. Some people are able to live off residual income generated from other investments such as real estate or a business they have built when they are no longer working. Many people have a combination of these.

A person who is close to retirement, or who has already retired, must make decisions and adjustments that will ensure they will continue to have enough to live on. The amount needed will depend on their lifestyle, the age at which they retire and how much debt they have. I have met with many retirees who have a large retirement income but, because of heavy debt, struggle financially. Columnist Earl Wilson has been quoted as saying, "There are three kinds of people: the haves, the have-nots, and the have-not-paid-for-what-they-haves."[4]

Most people who have financial difficulty during retirement didn't save enough, have too much debt or failed to do strategic planning to protect their investments. Remember what we discussed in chapter 1 about the last S in the acronym P.U.R.S.E.S., which stands for Security

System for Your Assets. While securing your assets is important at any stage of life, it is most critical in the retirement years. Why? Because most of the time, there will not be enough time to recover from losses. A thirty-year-old woman who losses 30 percent of her retirement savings due to a downturn in the market is in a far different situation than a woman who is sixty-five and suffers the same loss. The thirty-year-old has time for the market to recover before she needs the funds to live on. Many times the sixty-five-year-old is already in the distribution stage of life, taking an income from her investments.

From August 2007 to October 2008, an estimated 20 percent, or $2 trillion, disappeared from American retirement plans.[5] This had a profound effect on people who were on the verge of retirement or had already retired. Many of those who were planning to retire during that time period were forced to work another five years just to recoup their losses.

A vegetable garden may be growing nicely and producing a bountiful crop. Then, suddenly, without warning, a storm can come along and cause severe damage and loss. This is true for a person's financial portfolio as well. A money garden that took a lifetime to grow can be wiped out in a very short amount of time. Women must guard themselves against these devastating financial storms.

In the next chapter, we will discuss mistakes women make that cause them and their loved ones to suffer financial loss. Financial security can slip right through a person's fingers. Not only is it important to grow a portfolio, you must learn how to protect it. By learning how to avoid costly mistakes and building a strong plan that can weather a storm, a woman can feel secure about her financial future.

CHAPTER SUMMARY

1) Seven principles for growing a successful garden:

   PLOW. Time of preparation

   PLANT. Sowing seeds: time, labor, energy, money

   PRUNE. Weeding out what is overtaking dreams and goals

   PICK. Harvest time

   PRESERVE. Planning for tomorrow

   PASS. Giving to others

2) Money can offer:

   • Freedom from stress

   • Freedom from hectic lifestyles and undesirable chores

   • Freedom to travel

   • Freedom to spend more time with those you love

   • Freedom to do the things you want to do

   • Freedom to buy what you want when you want it

3) Four ways to make money:

   • Employee

- Self-Employed

- Business Owner

- Investor

4) Saving For Retirement

- Employer plans

- Self-Employed plans

- IRAs

5) Protecting the Money Garden

CHAPTER 6

Common Financial Mistakes Made By Women

Every woman has made mistakes during her lifetime; however, some mistakes are easier to recover from than others. Some financial mistakes can have long-lasting consequences, and pulling out of them can often be very difficult.

Through the years, I have witnessed the devastating effects that financial mistakes can have on women. I am passionate about helping them understand how to avoid unnecessary suffering caused by these mistakes. For that reason, I am going to boldly deal with some of the issues, even at the risk of sounding insensitive or even sarcastic. I realize that this chapter may cause some readers to feel uncomfortable. However, if I can help even a few women avoid these painful mistakes, it will be worth it.

Let's explore some of the most common mistakes women make when dealing with money and finances.

"People are motivated by either
inspiration or desperation."

Mistake #1. Spend Little or No Time Planning for Their Financial Future

Here is a list of five things that women usually spend much more time doing than planning for their financial future. While there is nothing inherently wrong with most of them, I find the imbalance of time and energy interesting.

1) **Shopping for unnecessary items.** While some shopping is necessary, women are relentless shoppers for a variety of reasons that have nothing to do with the necessities of life.

   Here are a few:

   Boredom/Entertainment. As women, I think it is almost impossible to deny that at some point in our lives, even if not on a regular basis, we have been guilty of this one. Women shop just for the sake of shopping. It is a fun way to spend time with girlfriends. Even when we are traveling or on vacation, we usually fit shopping into our itinerary, as a part of the entire experience. We purchase countless trinkets and souvenirs that we jam into our already packed-to-the-max suitcases and expend energy making sure everything arrives back home with us intact. Sadly, most of these items we spent so much time fussing over wind up in a yard sale or thrown in the trash. How do I know this? I have done it myself!

   Emotional Shopping. Have you ever thought to yourself, *I'm feeling a little down today. I know; I will go shopping!* Strolling through the mall can help distract us from the many issues we have to deal with in life. Ironically, the emotional shopping many women do is causing them to go further into debt, which can ultimately cause severe depression. Even if you can afford to shop emotionally, so much money can be spent on unnecessary items as we continue to pack more and more clothes, shoes and accessories in already bulging closets. Then we have to deal with where to put everything, which also causes us stress. In essence, emotional shopping really makes no sense at all. It is almost like substance abuse; it can cause a woman to feel better momentarily, but when the thrill is gone, the aftereffects can cause her to suffer even more.

Influenced by Advertisements. No matter how intelligent we are, we can easily be influenced by expert marketing that causes us to act in a fashion we had no prior intentions of doing. One-day sales, limited time offers, buy one/get one free, 25 percent off coupons, special interest rates (or no interest for a period of time) can certainly rev up our shopping engine. Millions of marketing dollars are spent to motivate shoppers to action. And guess what? They work like a charm! Smart shoppers should take advantage of money-saving opportunities when they apply to something they really need, but all too often these motivators cause us to make irrational decisions we can certainly regret later. One example is having to pay 25 percent interest because we did not make the interest-free deadline for paying off the debt.

The Markdown. I have found myself purchasing a blouse, suit or other article of clothing I needed like a hole in my head. Being able to purchase a suit for 25 to 50 percent of its original price seemed like a deal too good to pass up. Sometimes the items we purchase for this reason are barely (if ever) used because they really didn't fit, we never found the right occasion to wear them or we really didn't even like them that much in the first place. Crazy, isn't it?

The Other-People-Own-It, So-Should-I Syndrome. Think back… what have you purchased in the past that was the result of someone else owning it first? When we see an item that someone else has purchased, many times nothing will do but finding out exactly where they got it and seeing how quickly we can rush to the store to see if they have any more left of this amazing item.

Window Shopping. What a funny term. You would think it means you are shopping for a window, right? But we all know exactly what it means. We wander through the malls or other places that provide gorgeous displays meant to lure us into the stores. Store owners know that putting a beautiful outfit on a size two, five-foot-eight-inch mannequin is to a woman like displaying a large, juicy steak to a hungry animal. Our mouths began to water as we picture how wonderful that gorgeous outfit will look on us, most of us forgetting that we are not a size two. I have experienced the disappointment when I tried on an outfit that looked so sweet and wonderful on the thin mannequin, only to discover how differently it looked on me. It really made me feel a little sad!

Let me reiterate; shopping can be a fun and relaxing experience. Almost every woman loves to shop to one degree or another. If you have the money to treat yourself to a fun shopping trip, there is absolutely nothing wrong with it. However, when we spend all of our time spending money but no time learning how to make it, invest it or protect it, we will most likely find ourselves at some point not being able to shop 'til we drop because we lack the funds to do so.

2) **Concerning ourselves with the affairs of others.** This is another thing some women spend much of their time and

energy on. I am always amazed at how much information women have about other people in comparison to the amount of information they have regarding their own finances. Most women are creatures of communication. We love to share. As a result, we spend hours and hours sharing about our lives, and the lives of others, with one another. Most times, there is nothing wrong with this. We gain tremendous emotional support from one another. But once again, the time we spend talking back and forth with others is out of proportion with the time we spend securing our own financial futures, which is sometimes ignored altogether.

Sharing satisfies our need for emotional ties to one another. Dealing with finances is not nearly as satisfying during the process, but the benefits from taking the time to do so certainly will bring great rewards. Being financially stable ourselves can actually strengthen our emotional wellness, which can ultimately position us to be there for others, rather than having to cry on someone else's shoulder when we are suffering from our own lack of financial responsibility.

3) **Watching talk shows, reality shows and soaps.** Over the years, women have spent untold hours viewing and listening to the lives of others as they are played out on television. We get caught up in the issues, concerns and drama (even if fictitious) of others. I even heard the story of one lady who stood up in her church to request prayer for a couple who was getting a divorce. This sounds fine, until you realize that the couple she was requesting prayer for were actors on a soap opera! Are you guilty of spending more time focused on reality shows instead of thinking about your own reality: your financial future?

4) **Text messaging and e-mailing.** Modern technology has made it so easy for us to relate through cyberspace. Unfortunately, this has also created the opportunity for people to spend endless hours texting and e-mailing information that is more entertaining than necessary. Now, just so you'll know, I am not living in the dark ages. I do access my cell phone and computer daily. Both of these are convenient and efficient for the most part, both personally and in running my companies. However, most of my close friends know not to send me frivolous group e-mails; they understand that I do not take the time to read them.

This is not to reprimand anyone who spends time passing around information they feel might be useful or fun to their friends, which is completely harmless in and of itself. I am just using this as another example of things women spend many more hours doing than putting together a solid financial plan for the present as well as the future.

5) **Thinking about how they wish they were financially secure.** Enormous amounts of time are spent by women thinking about money and financial security. This may sound contradictory to what I have been saying, but it isn't. Notice, I used the word *thinking* about their finances, not doing anything about it. As a matter of fact, thinking is probably not even the right word; it's more like worrying about their finances. Many women have shared with me how they spend sleepless nights worrying about the market and other issues regarding their financial portfolios and situations. There is nothing productive about worry. It will not change your situation at all. Action is the only thing that will make any difference. Women who get proactive in securing their financial futures eliminate much stress in their lives.

Mistake #2. Being Uninformed or Misinformed about the Family Finances

For some married women, the first time they even begin to deal with finances is when their husbands pass away. As I mentioned earlier in this book, this is the worst time for a woman to have to face a new responsibility. I have met women who were in complete denial and would not even let themselves begin to deal with any financial matters after losing their husbands. Statements and bills sat on the counter for months, untouched. I've also seen women sit and weep so uncontrollably that they could not even get through a financial planning session. Not only was this very unfamiliar territory for them but at the same time they were overwhelmed with emotions that were still very raw from losing their spouses, some of whom had been married their entire adult lives.

I have personally helped women dig through filing cabinets searching for financial records. I remember one lady in Florida who, while we were searching, found an account statement that reflected a $50,000 balance she never knew about because her husband had always handled the money. On the other hand, I have met with women who were devastated to learn that accounts they thought they had did not even exist anymore, as a result of the money being spent, moved or lost in the market while their husbands were alive.

Whether you are married or single, and whether or not you are the one who handles the day-to-day affairs of your finances, let me strongly urge you to be informed at all times about your financial portfolio. I know this is going to sound harsh, but it is completely irresponsible to be uninformed or misinformed about such a vital part of your life and well-being.

Mistake #3. Think Money Isn't that Important as Long as They Have **LOVE.**

No matter how much love you have in your life, it will never negate the necessity for financial planning. While being loved is something almost every person desires, love does not pay the bills. Love will not keep you out of foreclosure. Love will not put food on the table, pay the utility bill or cover the cost of health care. Women are now, more than ever, beginning to understand the importance of being financially competent. A woman who has taken control of her own financial future can date or marry a man without having to choose someone who can take care of her financially. The relationship is born out of a true desire to spend time together, not to lean on someone for financial burden bearing.

Mistake #4. Their Investments and Spending Habits Are Not Aligned with Their Goals and Dreams.

Speaking with hundreds of women over the years who are retired or nearing retirement, I hear some of the same answers when I ask certain questions. For example, I many times ask the simple question, "What are your financial goals?" Although some look at me like they've never been asked such a complicated question, many women do come back with this answer: "I want to make sure my money is safe, and that I will always have enough to live on."

This certainly sounds like a reasonable goal for women, especially in the retirement stage of life; however, when I begin to examine their investment strategies and spending habits, they do not reflect the goal that has been communicated to me. Many times the same women who have said that safety of investments is one of their main priorities show me brokerage accounts that have the majority of their portfolio in highly risky investments with no guarantees. Other times I see women holding hundreds of thousands of dollars in bank accounts paying little or next to nothing in interest, which do not have a chance of keeping up with inflation and could ultimately cause a person to deplete all of their funds before they die.

Then there are women who, after communicating to me how important it is to have enough money for their lifetime, tell me of their enormous credit card debt. Many say that they did not see this coming. Little by little, they continued to charge items on their cards, and before they knew it, they had built up what seemed to be an insurmountable debt. Benjamin Franklin once said, "Beware of little expenses; a small leak will sink a great ship."[1]

Women who have a certain set of goals yet have investments and spending habits that will never help them reach those goals, can be likened to a person who wants to paint a wall blue but goes to the store and purchases a gallon of red paint. The goal of having a blue wall will never be achieved using red paint.

All of this goes back to having a Purpose Based Plan. Just having an array of investments, bank accounts and insurance products that are thrown together without a well-thought-out plan definitely does not suggest that financial goals will ever be met.

Mistake #5. Make Emotional Decisions about Money Instead of Logical Ones

Men and women can be vastly different when it comes to how they deal with money. Men are usually much more factual and have a higher risk tolerance. Women, on the other hand, are sometimes more emotional, relational and seek security. Here are a few observations comparing men and women and how they can differ in dealing with finances:

1) Men can look at an investment and be very interested in the numbers. Women tend to look at an investment and relate it to their lives: "Will I be taken care of with this investment?"

2) A man will determine if he wants to stay with a financial adviser based on how well the adviser has handled the portfolio. Most men have no problem walking away from an adviser who has done a poor job of handling their investments, even if the adviser is a friend. Men understand that it's just business. Women, on the other hand, may stay with an unproductive adviser, sometimes a person who had done a poor job handling their portfolio, because they don't want to hurt the person's feelings by leaving them. After all, they're such nice guys (or gals).

3) Even the way a woman spends money is usually different from a man. Women get excited about a sale or the experience of shopping. Most men shop for things they need, no big deal. Women also give money away out of emotion, such as caring for children, grandchildren, etc. Most men are far more reserved when it comes to bailing someone out.

Emotions are good, and they are certainly natural for women. However, women must use their heads more than their hearts in regard to handling finances. The time is now for women to get out their pencils and paper and began to formulate and activate a plan that is built on logic and facts rather than letting emotions take the helm and eventually keep them from ever reaching their desired financial destination.

Mistake #6. Sometimes Live in Financial La-la Land

As I said in the introduction of this book, there are many women who are astute in finances. In no way am I saying that these mistakes paint a picture of all women suffering from deficiencies regarding financial planning. But I have vast experience dealing with women and how they handle money. While more and more women are embracing the idea of being financially savvy, there are still many who are living in a financial la-la land.

Wandering through life with your head in the sand regarding any subject always holds risks and dangers, including being in financial la-la land. Financial land mines are hidden everywhere and can be ignited unexpectedly. One wrong step and you can set off an explosion that can be devastating, causing extreme financial damage that is many times irreparable.

Living in denial or sticking your head in the sand does not make the land mines go away. Women who are responsible and take ownership of their financial futures can greatly insure themselves against the potential threats that may be hiding in financial la-la land.

Mistake #7. Do Not Have a Basic Understanding of Money, Investments and Asset Protection

The U in P.U.R.S.E.S. stands for Understanding Money Basics. While it is unnecessary and certainly not feasible for every woman to become a financial planner, just as all women cannot become doctors, women should at least get a basic understanding of how money works and the resources that are available to them, thus avoiding what could be a financial calamity.

In recent years, women have become more knowledgeable and proactive with health management issues. Today, more than ever, women are taking the time to understand the steps and information needed to insure a healthier, longer life. Many deaths are being avoided due to women taking better care of themselves and engaging in preventive care, exams and screenings.

Just as health issues can impair a person from enjoying their retirement years, so can being unprepared financially. The fact that you are taking the time to read this book is an indicator that you are being proactive in securing your financial future.

Mistake #8. Unintentionally Put Heavy Burdens on Their Children: Taxation, Long-Term Care and Settling Estates

In the coming chapters, I will address these issues in further detail. But for now, let me just say this: most mothers would do anything to keep their children from feeling pain or experiencing any unpleasantness or stress. However, because of a lack of planning, they may inadvertently cause their children to:

1) Pay capital gains taxes unnecessarily because they did not take advantage of the step-up provision.

2) Pay federal estate taxes unnecessarily. These can be astronomical if a portion of the estate is not exempt.

3) Be responsible for their long-term care because of inadequate savings, lack of insurance or becoming ineligible for Medicaid assistance.

4) Deal with the grueling tasks and stress of settling an estate, which can take months or even years to complete.

The thing that is so sad about this is the fact that with just a bit of planning and forethought, so many of these problems can be avoided. If you care about your children, or whomever your heirs may be, let me implore you to be responsible and put an estate plan in order to eliminate these burdens.

Mistake #9. Don't Believe Their Estate Is Large Enough for an Estate Plan

Many people misunderstand the meaning of the word *estate*. As a result, they get the impression that unless they have enormous wealth, they have no need for estate planning. Some have been told by well-meaning friends, relatives and even professionals that they do not need an estate plan.

In its simplest form, an estate can mean a possession or ownership. Most people do have some sort of possessions—home, accounts, land or other items. Granted, some estates require more extensive, sophisticated planning than others; however, everyone should spend some time deciding on how their estate will pass to their heirs and take whatever steps are necessary to ensure this passing is done in an efficient manner.

Estate planning will be discussed in greater detail in chapter 10.

Mistake #10. Have Unsuitable Insurance Policies

Insurance is rarely considered a mistake. Not having it can sometimes be disastrous. However, it is imperative to own the right type and amount of insurance for your particular stage of life. In addition, it is important to consider who is named as the insured, the beneficiary and the owner of policies.

When we have minor children, life insurance is usually an extremely important consideration. As we move to middle age and beyond, the purpose of using insurance products can drastically change. Life insurance can certainly be useful for spousal income replacement during retirement years when a spouse passes away and his/her pension decreases or ends completely.

However, some women are continuing to pay premiums on policies that are no longer serving their original purpose. I have met women who are paying premiums on life insurance policies that aren't really needed while they struggle to pay their bills because of inadequate income. In chapter 8, we will discuss how a person can potentially turn an old insurance policy into income.

Mistake #11. Trip Over a Hundred-Dollar Bill to Pick Up a Nickel

Finding a $100 bill in an empty parking lot would be exciting, to say the least. How many of us would ignore that valuable bill only to run to secure a shiny new nickel we spotted just a few feet away? Not many, right? Yet this is exactly what many people do day after day. They take extreme measures to make sure they get to use a 25-percent-off coupon, yet ignore the high interest rates being charged on unpaid credit-card balances. Or some people spend loads of time and energy checking out all of the CD interest rates to decide where they can get another one-quarter or one-half percent, yet pay hundreds, perhaps even thousands, in unnecessary taxes.

Ladies, grab hold of the financial benefits of good, solid financial planning. Don't let the savings of a few measly bucks rob you of the time needed to put your estate and retirement plan on the right track. Get serious. While there is nothing wrong with using coupons or shopping for the best interest rates on CDs, when you ignore the big picture, you truly are tripping over a $100 bill to pick up a nickel.

Mistake #12. Procrastination

As mentioned in a prior chapter, too many women live on Someday Isle: someday I'll do this, someday I'll do that. Have you ever had an item on your to-do list that you just kept putting off? Almost everyone can think of one or more things we know we should get done, but we just keep procrastinating. Here's one thing I know:

"PEOPLE ARE MOTIVATED BY EITHER INSPIRATION OR DESPERATION."

Unfortunately, many people are never moved to action until they are in a desperate situation. That's the very reason I meet so many recently widowed women. Many of them have spent a lifetime avoiding dealing with finances. Then they are thrust into having to face the reality of their new financial responsibilities and are, therefore, desperate for help.

Many people intended to get long-term care insurance, but because they put it off and an unexpected accident or an illness such as Alzheimer's or stroke occurred during the procrastination period, they suffered irreversible financial devastation.

Even though people know legal documents, such as a will or trust, are important for settling an estate, many put it off until it is too late, ultimately leaving their family with a mess that could take years to deal with.

Do not delay until tomorrow, for tomorrow never comes.

Mistake #13. Believe that Life Will Always Look the Way It Does Today

For some strange reason, many women see the rest of their lives as being exactly the same as it currently is. If they are married, they don't really think too much about not having a spouse at some point in the future. If they are healthy, they don't picture themselves ever dealing with physical disabilities. If they are wealthy, they cannot imagine not having enough money.

This type of thinking is very unrealistic, but it accounts for why many women are not motivated to take financial planning seriously. As I mentioned before, there are a great number of people who think they will always find themselves in the positive percentage of statistics. Unfortunately, that type of attitude can be exactly why they will land on the negative side. While they revel in the good fortune of their present lives, they forget the importance of planning ahead.

Many who think there is only clear sailing ahead are very shocked when dark clouds gather and quickly turn blue skies and calm winds into a storm that wreaks havoc on their ship of life, causing them to drift far from their intended destination.

Mistake #14. Have a Portfolio that Does Not Fit and Is Not Age Appropriate

I realize that there are some women who do not like to reveal their age. I am not one of those women. I gladly blurt out my age to anyone who is interested. I almost see it as quite an achievement to have made it to the age I am, considering some of the things I have been through in my life.

But whether you are a tell-all kind of woman like me, or you prefer to leave your age undisclosed, one of the areas in which your age should be reflected is your portfolio. I never cease to be amazed at how many women who are in their sixties have a portfolio that reflects that of someone in their thirties.

We have all seen women who wear clothes that either don't fit or are inappropriate for their age. Let me just say that, in my opinion, it is not cool for a seventy-five-year-old to wear a miniskirt. Along those same lines, wearing clothes that are three sizes too small can be just as disturbing to those who have to see it.

The reason many women wind up with a financial catastrophe is that they never made necessary adjustments to their portfolio as they got older. Normally, this is a result of not paying enough attention to their investments or assuming their financial adviser was taking care of necessary changes for them. While some advisers frequently review their clients' portfolios, there are others who put the investments on autopilot and only make changes when the client initiates them.

Please *do not* ever assume that having a financial adviser eliminates your need for involvement in your own financial planning. Many, many women who had an adviser in charge of their portfolio during the recession found themselves with huge losses due to investments that carried far too much risk for where they were in life.

Picking investments is like shopping for clothes. You should find the ones that fit well and are the appropriate style for your age.

Mistake #15. Have a Portfolio that Is Too Complicated

Most portfolios need to be diversified; however, that does not mean they must be complicated. Many women do not understand the difference. Some women believe that the more complicated their investments, the more diversified they are. This is simply not true.

Henry David Thoreau, famous American author and philosopher, said, "Our life is frittered away by detail. Simplify, simplify."[2]

I once had a lady tell me that she just wanted her financial adviser to let her know how much money she had made since he had taken over her portfolio. She asked him, "How many nuts did I give you and how many nuts do I have now?" I thought this was an excellent question. Unfortunately, she told me that he could never give her a straight answer. This seems odd to me. Perhaps he was just attempting to avoid the question.

People have a right to know how their investments have performed. This should be a priority to women, not how impressive their fifty-page brokerage statement looks. Interestingly enough, some brokerage statements only reflect the performance of a portfolio in the year it began to rise.

Something I do when I am meeting with one of my clients for a review is to give them an Account Summary Sheet. Basically, this is a summary of how much money they invested at the very beginning, how many withdrawals they have taken and the value of the account to date. These numbers quickly reveal the performance of their account. Rather than maneuvering through years of statements, they can quickly see how many nuts they gave me to invest, and how many nuts they have now. Makes sense, right?

The type of investment you have will determine how often a company is required to send you a detailed statement. Details are good. Just make sure you don't get so bogged down in the details that you don't understand the overall performance of your investments. Most statements will include both details and a summary of your account.

Mistake #16. Lack of Organization

Over the years, I have met with a great many women who began our first appointment by bringing in boxes, bags and even laundry baskets crammed full of statements, policies and various other important documents. In order to give someone sound financial advice, you must first understand where they are financially. Unfortunately, many women are so disorganized, they don't even know themselves.

Some women are not only in a fog about what their financial picture looks like but they waste untold amounts of hours digging through piles of papers, another example of devaluing their time.

Mistake #17. Don't Maximize Income Opportunities

Having enough income is usually very high on a woman's priority list; however, many women are not taking advantage of assets and accounts that could be used for income. Since chapter 8 will offer specific advice on income planning, I will not spend much time on this issue at this point. But it is important to note that this particular mistake is causing women to have much less income than is possible, even when they have already moved into retirement.

Another place where this mistake is more apparent is not taking advantage of their unique gifts and talents. They settle for jobs that pay less than those they are actually qualified for.

Mistake # 18. Seek Advice from Unqualified People

Some of the stories I have heard over the years from women telling me why they decided to make certain financial decisions based on advice from well-meaning but highly unqualified friends or family have made me cringe. I think to myself, *wow… just wow!*

Let's stop and take a moment to ponder this. Why would a woman take advice on such a serious subject as finances from someone who is unqualified? If a person needs heart surgery, would they seek advice from a CPA? A woman who is considering selling her home would not solicit advice from the paperboy. You get my point!

Yet scores of women have made very important financial decisions based on a recommendation from an unqualified person: a cousin's boyfriend's sister's son who once took an economics class. Yikes! While I am being somewhat facetious, I have truly heard stories that are that crazy.

Mistake #19. Overpay Taxes

Chapter 9 will discuss tax planning in detail, but for now, let me just say that overpayment of taxes is a huge mistake people many times overlook. One of the fastest ways to become a more ingenious investor is to minimize taxes. Does this mean committing tax fraud? Absolutely not! But why pay taxes you don't really owe? Many people pay hundreds, even thousands or tens of thousands of dollars in unnecessary taxes.

Mistake #20. Take Unnecessary Risks

Mark Twain once said, "October: This is one of the peculiarly dangerous months to speculate in stocks. The others are July, January, September, April, November, May, March, June, December, August and February."[3]

Many people have made large sums of money by investing in stocks. Therefore, of course, it makes sense for some people. But this should be determined by your age, risk tolerance and overall financial portfolio.

Ask yourself the question, Do I really need risky investments? Perhaps you have already accumulated a nice portfolio. Securing what you have could make more sense than continuing to expose your assets to volatile market conditions.

If investing in the market seems to be a good fit for you, just make sure you have time to recover if there is a sharp decline. The biggest single-day loss in the history of the Dow occurred on September 29,

2008, when it dropped 777.68 points, or approximately $1.2 trillion in market value. In that same year, U.S. households lost an estimated 18 percent of their net worth, approximately $11.2 trillion. This collapse was the largest since the Federal Reserve began tracking household wealth after World War II.[4]

Many people were hit hard at that time, including retirees. Some retirees had to go back to work. Others, who were within a few months or even days of retiring, had to remain in the workforce for several more years. Much of this could have been avoided by older adults if they had been more proactive in securing their portfolio in age-appropriate investments instead of exposing themselves to unnecessary risks.

Mistake #21. Fail to Protect Themselves from Catastrophic Events

Going back to the acronym, P.U.R.S.E.S., you will recall that the last S stands for Security System for Your Assets. When something is valuable, we want to protect it; that is why we insure it. We insure our homes, cars, jewelry, etc. However, sometimes we forget to insure ourselves against the many hurricanes that can wipe out a portfolio it has taken a lifetime to build. We must learn to build a thick wall of protection so that we can feel secure no matter what events may take place in our lives.

Mistake #22. Spend Money They Don't Have to Buy Things They Don't Need to Impress People They Don't Like!

Okay, to lighten things up a bit, this one is thrown in here for fun. Even so, it is a true statement. If you are guilty of doing this, always remember the 20/40/60 rule: At twenty years old, women are worried to death about what other people think of them; at forty, they don't really care what people think of them; at age sixty, they finally realize that no one has been thinking about them all along.

Seriously, though, all of the aforementioned financial mistakes made by women can certainly be avoided. Interestingly enough, it really doesn't take that much time or effort to prevent these mistakes from being made.

Mistakes can destroy your money garden. Just like a hurricane or tornado can quickly cause severe damage and loss, financial mistakes can certainly have the same effect on your financial portfolio.

If you have already made some of these mistakes, you must do what a person does when hazardous weather has taken a toll on their property. Here are five steps you should take:

1) Assess the damage

2) Take inventory of what is left

3) Reevaluate and redesign your plan

4) Begin implementing your new plan

5) Start the recovery process

Everyone makes mistakes. How you deal with them and learning to avoid them in the future will make all the difference in the world when moving toward financial security. In chapter 11, we will discuss three important steps that will lead to change.

It is my desire that as you continue reading this book, the information within will motivate and inspire you to get your financial household in order. Learn from your past and plan for your future. This will make life for yourself and your loved ones much easier.

CHAPTER SUMMARY

22 Financial Mistakes Made By Women

1) Spend Little or No Time Planning for Their Financial Future

2) Being Uninformed or Misinformed about the Family Finances

3) Think Money Is Unimportant; They Just Need *Love*

4) Their Investments and Spending Habits Are Not Aligned With Their Goals and Dreams

5) Make Emotional Decisions about Money Instead of Logical Ones

6) Live in Financial La-la Land

7) Do Not Have a Basic Understanding of Money, Investments and Asset Protection

8) Unintentionally Put Heavy Burdens on Their Children: Taxation, Long-Term Care and Settling Estates

9) Don't Believe that Their Estate Is Large Enough for an Estate Plan

10) Have Unsuitable Insurance Policies

11) Trip Over a Hundred-Dollar Bill to Pick Up a Nickel

12) Procrastination

13) Believe that Life Will Always Look the Way It Does Today

14) Have a Portfolio that Does Not Fit and Is Not Age-Appropriate

15) Have a Portfolio That Is Too Complicated

16) Lack of Organization

17) Don't Maximize Income Opportunities

18) Seek Advice from Unqualified People

19) Overpay Taxes

20) Take Unnecessary Risks

21) Fail to Protect Themselves from Catastrophic Events

22) Spend Money They Don't Have to Buy Things They Don't Need to Impress People They Don't Like

PART II

A Financial Plan

CHAPTER 7

Eight Characteristics of a Strong Financial Plan

Many people feel that if they get a legal document set up, such as a will, and choose a few investments, they have created a solid financial and estate plan. While this is definitely a part of planning, it doesn't end there. Without a well-thought-out Purpose Based Plan, a person can find herself with a flimsy, inefficient plan that is weak and quickly falls apart with the least little puff of wind.

Remember the story of the Three Little Pigs? Although each pig had built a house for himself, there was only one whose house was built with the strength to keep the big, bad wolf from blowing the house down. Many financial and estate plans look good on the outside. Scores of women are walking around with a false sense of security that their current plan is going to shelter them and their heirs from financial calamity. Unfortunately, when the puffs of life come along, many women find themselves with a plan that was not built with the strength and endurance to weather the storm. Many financial storms cause severe damage and sometimes totally annihilate a financial and estate plan that was built with a faulty structure.

Do not leave yourself or your
family without options.

Some of these storms, or hurricanes as we referred to them in previous chapters, include loss of income, market losses, taxes, probate, cost of nursing home care and even lawsuits. Some have the potential of wiping out your money garden in one big storm. Others are more like bugs and insects that subtly eat away at your garden little by little until nothing is left.

With this in mind, let's look at some strong plans that work.

A WRITTEN PLAN

Women have actually told me that they have simply given their children verbal instructions on how to handle their estate; they did not bother setting up any type of legal documents. Ladies, this is wrong on so many levels!

First of all, when you do not have legal documents in place, anything can happen. Even when you do have documents drawn up, desires and wishes may never result in the way you had intended. We will discuss this possibility in chapter 10. For now, let me just say, please do some basic estate planning at a minimum.

So many women are under the false impression that their children would never argue or fight over settling their estate. For some, this may be true. But one never knows how their loved ones will react in any given situation. Sometimes an argument over one simple item can drag out for months or even years. This is not only inefficient but many times relationships suffer irreparable emotional damage during this process. Why put your heirs in danger of this possibility?

Furthermore, spouses of your children can certainly be influencers in these types of matters, causing your loved ones to make irrational decisions that they would not have otherwise made. The risk of these types of problems is just not worth it. These issues can certainly be avoided with the correct written plan.

Not only should you have legal documents that will simplify the process of estate planning but you must also have a written plan that will help guide you to your goals while you are living. In chapter 12, we will discuss how you can develop a written plan that will serve as a financial roadmap.

AN UPDATED PLAN

In my opinion, an estate plan needs to be reviewed at least once every five years, no matter what. In addition, a plan should be updated when any of the following occurrences take place: you move to another state, you purchase or sell major assets or your beneficiaries change.

Compare your estate plan to your wardrobe. Women naturally update their wardrobe constantly. Why? Because some things don't fit anymore, your fashion desires change or your old wardrobe is outdated. We want to make our clothes and accessories conform to our current needs and desires. So it is with our estate plan. Some of the items in our old plans just don't fit our current situation. I have seen estate plans where the beneficiaries are no longer living but no one has been named in their place. Also, when it has been years since a person updated her plan, the provisions may not make sense anymore. An example of this would be a person who has not updated her plan since her children were minors; now her children are grown with their own children.

We know that it is necessary to routinely go for medical checkups and exams. Just because we had a mammogram one time certainly does not negate the need for another one in the future. If we are acting responsibly, we will continue our checkups routinely. We should also take this same approach to making sure our current estate plan is up to speed. To neglect doing so is irresponsible.

A COORDINATED PLAN

Most women do not understand the value of a coordinated plan. As a matter of fact, most people do not possess this type of plan. Without it, a person will forfeit the enormous financial benefits it provides. What exactly is a coordinated plan? It is one that has been carefully constructed making each piece fit together to maximize and enhance the entire picture, rather than negatively affecting the other pieces.

Let me explain: If your financial adviser has chosen investments for you that are causing you a large tax burden, your financial plan may not be coordinated with a good tax plan. Have you ever gone to see your CPA feeling pretty good about the performance of your portfolio that year only to learn of a huge tax liability you now owe?

Your professional advisers should be working together on some level to ensure that your overall plan fits together, creating the ultimate benefit for you, the client. If this type of attention to detail is being neglected by one of your advisers, perhaps you need to look elsewhere to find a team player whose goal is to maximize all possibilities of financial advantage for you.

THE RIGHT PLAN

Females are notorious for seeing what someone else has done and following suit. While this is relatively harmless in most areas, such as purchasing a particular item that someone else had first or picking the same vacation spot after a friend came home raving about it, setting up the same estate plan just because it was right for someone else is usually a bad choice. Why? Well, think about it for a moment. Rarely, if ever, do two different families have all of the exact same assets, income, family structure and goals for passing on assets. While an estate plan may resemble that of someone you know, there is still the need for customizing it to create a perfect fit for you. If your friend shows you a beautiful size 10 dress she has just purchased, and you are motivated to buy one for yourself, it would be crazy to purchase a size 10 when you are a size 6. Even though you are looking for a duplicate of the dress, you would certainly purchase the one that fits you, not your friend.

Once again, if you take the time to put together a Purpose Based Plan, you will most likely come up with the right plan for you, one that takes into consideration your unique situation, needs and desires.

A COMPLETE PLAN

Make sure that every area of your financial and estate plan has been addressed. Leaving out just one of the important aspects of your plan can affect all the rest. Three areas that must be included in a strong plan are income planning, tax planning and estate planning, all of which will be discussed in detail in the chapters that follow. In my experience, women rarely address all of them properly. While some have worked diligently on income and estate plans, their lack of tax planning has a negative effect on the overall plan, drastically reducing what heirs will receive after she passes on. Others expend great effort toward tax and estate planning but fail to recognize maximum income potential due to poor income planning.

Just as leaving out a key ingredient for a recipe can change the entire taste of the dish you are preparing, leaving out an important aspect of your financial and estate plan can change the entire landscape of your portfolio.

AN IMPLEMENTED PLAN

Have you ever started something you did not finish? Of course we all have. However, some unfinished projects have far less severe consequences than others. An incomplete estate plan can result in serious financial repercussions for you as well as your heirs.

Some people own a beautifully bound, professional-looking Revocable Living Trust binder with very official documents inside. However, because they never completed the funding of the trust, it is like an empty bucket that contains nothing and can be rendered completely useless in transferring assets to heirs. In many cases when an attorney draws up a trust, he does not take on the task of funding the trust, especially without an additional fee. Although an attorney should make it crystal clear that an unfunded trust will not function properly, there are still many people who unknowingly possess an empty trust. This can be the result of a misunderstanding, miscommunication or both. Either way, people are stunned when they find out the ramifications of an incomplete estate plan.

In some cases, a client understood perfectly the importance of funding the trust but just never got around to it. Funding a trust is a fairly easy process done through notifying the institutions that are handling your accounts, letting them know you have a trust and that you'd like to rename your accounts into the trust. Most institutions will let you know the documents they need to fulfill your request. Because some accounts should not be owned by the trust, such as qualified retirement accounts, you must be careful not to change ownership for the wrong accounts, which can result in creating a taxable event. Using a professional to help you fund your trust is always a good idea to help you avoid these types of costly mistakes.

Don't be afraid to spend a little money to have a qualified professional assist you with a good estate plan. Some women absolutely refuse to pay a professional for this type of valuable service but have no qualms about spending hundreds of dollars on overpriced beauty products, designer clothes, purses, shoes and other temporary pleasures. Be responsible first, then go play.

A FLEXIBLE PLAN

In chapter 6, we discussed thinking her current situation will never change as one of the mistakes women make. Even though most people would be quick to agree that no one can predict the future, some plans I have reviewed over the years do not reflect that.

Many people have a financial plan that appears to be very strong. However, when the winds of change come, the plan snaps due to its inability to bend.

Let me give you an example: Many women (and men) have set up a plan based on a certain spouse passing away first. Their reasoning for this is usually based on age or health issues. Their entire plan is built on that assumption. I've even had women tell me that since they know their husbands will predecease them, they never felt the need to plan for anything else.

Unfortunately, there are times when the younger or more healthy spouse passes away first. For a family with an inflexible plan, this can leave the surviving spouse struggling financially for the rest of his or her life.

Another example is when a woman has made no provision for long-term care. Many women tell me that their children are their long-term care plan. However, when grown children are incapable of providing that care due to full-time jobs, lack of medical training, etc., a woman may find herself needing an assisted-living situation or even a nursing home without the funds to pay for it.

Hope for the best, but be prepared for the worst. One never knows what is around life's corners. Make sure your plan is flexible enough to bend with any situation that may come your way.

A PLAN THAT WORKS FOR BOTH LIFE AND DEATH

Believe it or not, most people have not planned for both of these. First, we have the group who only plans for dying. They have every detail of their death planned out, including prepaid funeral arrangements, burial plots, life insurance and a will. Many of these folks have their funeral ceremony written out in great detail, including desired songs and a requested speaker. While it is admirable to have the foresight to delve into this type of planning, many of these individuals wind up living twenty years or longer than they anticipated. Because their planning is focused solely on dying, they have no good financial plan for living so long and wind up running out of money way too soon.

On the other hand, there are those who plan to live forever; they haven't bothered to put any type of plan in place for dying, including legal documents and life insurance. When they do pass away, their heirs may have an awful mess to clean up while trying to settle their estate. This can sometimes take years. Not only does this lack of planning require enormous amounts of time and stress on the part of the heirs, many times the estate is eaten up in taxes and legal fees.

Here is another old cliché to share: a chain is only as strong as its weakest link. If any one of these eight areas we have discussed is weak, your plan could fall apart. Be responsible. Taking a little time to deal with these matters can save yourself and your heirs what is sometimes enormous amounts of loss, worry, grief and stress. Do not leave yourself or your family without options.

CHAPTER SUMMARY

Eight Characteristics of a Strong Financial Plan:

- A Written Plan

- An Updated Plan

- A Coordinated Plan

- The Right Plan

- A Complete Plan

- An Implemented Plan

- A Flexible Plan

- A Plan That Works for Both Life and Death

CHAPTER 8

Income Planning

As mentioned in chapter 7, there are three components that make up a well-constructed financial plan: income planning, tax planning and estate planning. If one of these is missing, there is a hole in the plan. Income planning will be our focus in this chapter.

A woman must devise a plan for how she will receive income at all stages of her life. Her plan must include present as well as future income. Many adjustments will have to be made along the way based on employment opportunities, investments and retirement goals.

Previously, we discussed the four ways people receive income: employee, self-employed, business owner and investor. So that you will have all the pieces necessary to put together your income plan, let's explore the different types, in three categories: temporary income, variable income and lifetime income.

TEMPORARY INCOME

Examples of temporary income include wages from employment, loan repayment and spousal income.

Annuities have become a
popular choice by many.

Why do we consider these temporary? Wages can only be counted on while a person is working, but most people do not work their entire lives. At some point, people leave the workforce and retire. Before retirement, their work patterns vary greatly. Some people have the same job for forty or more years, though this is becoming less and less common.

A study conducted over twenty-five years by the U.S. Bureau of Labor Statistics tracked the employment histories of 9,964 workers who were fourteen to twenty-two when first interviewed and thirty-nine to forty-eight when interviewed last. It found that the average younger boomer had held 10.5 jobs throughout his/her career. That works out to a job change about every two and one-third years. A job was defined as an "uninterrupted period of work with a particular employer." A promotion or change of position within a company was not counted as a different job.[1]

Some people, while changing jobs, go directly from one job to another. Others have big gaps in between jobs. Perhaps a woman takes time off to have a baby and be a stay-at-home mom for several years. Some women leave a job involuntarily because a company is downsizing or has other reasons for no longer wanting to offer her employment. Income can be interrupted many times when a person leaves a company to begin her own business. Months, sometimes even years, pass before income is generated again.

Another example of temporary income is a loan repayment by someone who owes you money. Some people hold the mortgage for a person who has purchased a home or business from them. When that loan is repaid, the income stops. Many people get used to living on the monthly income from someone who is repaying a loan to them. They forget that at some point that income will cease to exist.

Finally, spousal income should be considered temporary. Why? It can stop abruptly, or at least decrease greatly, after such life events as divorce, disability or death. Many women who always counted on the income from a spouse have been devastated when the spouse decided they wanted a divorce or died suddenly. If that spouse was receiving an income from their job or business, the income may come to a screeching halt. When a spouse who has been receiving Social Security and/or a pension passes away, the surviving spouse will more than likely see a drastic reduction in household income. Many pensions are stopped or reduced by half or more when the recipient dies. Social Security benefits end for that person as well.

Many women will have a long, happy marriage and enjoy the income from her spouse for most of her lifetime. However, if you happen to fall into one of the less favorable statistics we discussed in chapter 2, are you financially prepared to handle the situation?

VARIABLE INCOME

Variable income is subject to go up or down based on certain conditions and situations, including interest on investments, rental income and employment.

Let's begin with interest on investments. Over the past few years, people had CDs come due that were paying 5 percent in interest. When they went to renew those CDs, they found that banks were only offering ½ or 1 percent on the same investment. Many people will recall the time they were getting far more than 5 percent on their CDs. The interest rates change based on the economy.

Many of my clients own real estate. This source of income can vary greatly depending on the occupancy of tenants. People receiving rental income can see monthly changes of thousands of dollars as people move in and out of their properties.

Wages from employment or earnings from a business can be listed as variable as well as temporary income. Wages can be decreased when a person's hours are cut or they are demoted. A business owner's earnings can be sporadic based on sales and other success factors.

The point is that when you are putting together an income plan, these facts must be taken into consideration. A person who is working on a good financial plan would be remiss to overlook them. You must have a back-up plan that would compensate for reduced or loss of income due to temporary or variable situations. If not, you could find yourself struggling financially. Chapter 12 will offer some good suggestions on how to reinforce your financial plan.

LIFETIME INCOME

The third type of income is considered lifetime income. In other words, this income should last you for the duration of your life: Social Security, pensions and other annuities. While Social Security has been considered a reliable source of lifetime income, many people now doubt they will ever reap the benefits from this source.

U.S. News & World Report had this to say, "Social Security is often in the news these days. Congress regularly threatens to change and possibly reduce benefits. The program's financial soundness is the source of constant speculation and concern. And the economic downturn shone a light on the fact that more than half of all retirees depend on Social Security benefits for more than 90 percent of their income—an alarmingly high percentage for a program designed to provide modest retirement support."[2]

Some retirees count on their pensions for lifetime income. When a person retires from her job, she may be entitled to a pension that will pay her a steady income for the remainder of her life. A company purchases an annuity, normally a SPIA (Single Premium Immediate Annuity) when the person retires and dumps a one-time payment (or premium) into the annuity, which immediately begins to generate income for the retiree.

These annuities can be set up in a variety of ways. However, once an election is chosen, it cannot be changed. Normally, the three options for a SPIA are:

1) **Life Only.** This election insures that the payments will continue through the lifetime of the annuitant/owner, no matter how long he or she may live. However, once that person passes away, the payments stop. While this option normally has the highest payout, the trade-off is that if a person has received the payments for a very short amount of time when he or she dies, the payments end and there is no lump sum or continued payment for a surviving spouse or beneficiaries.

2) **Joint and Survivor.** Some married couples choose this option because they prefer a lifetime payout guaranteed for both lives. In this type of annuity, if one person passes away, the surviving spouse will continue to receive payments for the duration of their life. The payment will either be the same or a reduced amount for the surviving spouse based on the election that was made when the annuity was set up.

3) **Life With a Period Certain.** This annuity provides a lifetime payout for the annuitant/owner; however, if that person dies before a certain period has ended, payments will continue through that period to a named beneficiary. An example would

be a Life Annuity with a 10 Year Period Certain. This annuity would continue for the lifetime of the annuitant/owner. However, if that person dies before ten years has passed, a beneficiary would receive payments of the same amount for the remainder of the ten-year period. Once the ten years have passed, the payments end. No lump sum payment is ever available.

Unfortunately, many retirees choose the wrong option. Although sometimes this is the result of poor communication from the person explaining the options, most of the time it is because the retiree made a bad prediction about the future. Some people choose a life-only option because it will have the highest monthly payout. They may think that they will outlive their spouse based on age or health issues. However, as we've seen, an older spouse, or the one who had health issues, may outlive the person receiving the pension, resulting in the surviving spouse struggling to have enough income.

Many companies no longer offer pensions. Employer plans such as 401ks or 403bs have replaced pension options for many employees. In a few cases employers still offer both: a pension and an employer plan.

UNDERSTANDING ANNUITIES

Retirees who no longer have a pension must carefully decide what to do with the funds from their company plan to create their own form of lifetime income. That is one of the reasons annuities have become a popular choice by many.

An annuity can provide lifetime income, no matter how long a person lives. Annuities can only be purchased from life insurance companies. An annuity is a contract between the owner of the annuity and the insurance company. When using an annuity for creating lifetime income, the owner pays a certain amount of premium into the annuity, and, in exchange, the insurance company makes lifetime payments to the owner based on the value of the account and the age of the insured. The risk for the insurance company is that if the insured individual lives for a very long time and the funds in the account have been exhausted through annuity payments, the insurance company must continue to make payments through the end of the annuitant's life. In essence, the company is taking a risk that the insured will live too long. Life insurance works the opposite; the insurance company is taking the risk that the insured will die too soon.

There are many types of annuities. The SPIA is the one some people choose; however, for those who are more interested in their heirs receiving the lump sum of money that may be left in their account, a SPIA would not be the right choice.

Insurance companies have become very creative in designing modern-day annuities. Many offer annuities that allow for lifetime income and still pass a lump sum on to heirs. Some annuities accommodate charges that a person may incur from moving their investments by offering an upfront bonus.

There are three basic categories for annuities: fixed, indexed and variable. In the past several years indexed annuities have soared in popularity, especially in the fifty+ age group. This is mostly due to the fact that they have a higher earning potential than fixed annuities without the risk of loss due to market decline associated with variable annuities. Earnings are based on a market index such as the S & P 500 or NASDAQ. During the market disaster in 2008, no one suffered losses in an indexed annuity due to sharp decline in indices. In addition, when the market started back on an upward swing, most owners of indexed annuities had no ground to make up, because earnings are normally locked in on an annual basis.

Many financial advisers are quick to point out to their clients when their investments make 25 percent in one year; however, they usually do not bring up the fact that they lost 30 percent the year before. This may be a good time to ask your adviser, "How many nuts did I originally give you, and how many nuts do I have now?" Again, the beauty of the indexed annuity is no losses due to downturns of the market.

With an index annuity, which is a fairly conservative investment, there is usually a cap, spread or participation rate that should be considered. These can result in a limit on how much a person can earn each year in their annuity; however, when the account locks in the earnings each year and never has to make up a loss, these annuities many times outperform other investments, especially during years of sharp declines in the market, as we experienced after 9/11 and the recession of 2007–2009.

Fixed annuities are fairly simple to understand. You simply put your money into the annuity and a certain amount of fixed interest is paid each year. In recent years, these annuities have not been as popular as they once were because of declining interest rates. People are not willing to put their money into a long-term account with no potential for a higher return during the duration of the annuity.

Although an index annuity can be termed a fixed, indexed annuity, it has the potential of higher earnings through index strategy options.

A variable annuity is quite different from fixed or indexed annuities. With it, a person owns mutual funds, which can fluctuate based on market conditions; the value can go up or down. During consecutive years of a bull market, these annuities can soar in value; however, if the market declines, so will the value of the variable annuity. Some variable annuities offer options that will lock in gains, but, these options will require the owner of the annuity to pay a fee. The fees within a variable annuity can quickly add up, depending on how many options you choose. Total payment of fees can easily range from 2.5 to 4 percent. This sometimes includes the expense of the mutual funds within the annuity.

Almost all annuities have what is called a surrender period. This is the length of time that a penalty can be charged if too much of the annuity is withdrawn at one time. A typical annuity surrender period normally lasts seven to ten years; however, some are shorter and others are longer. Most annuities allow for a free withdrawal each year; the standard is 10 percent.

Penalties have scared people away from investing in annuities in the past. However, when a person understands how a penalty works, they are normally not as afraid of them. Let's compare a penalty within an annuity with one in a typical CD. In most cases if you invest $50,000 in a CD and you need $6,000 from the CD, you will need to cash in the CD and a penalty will be charged on the entire amount of the value of the CD, even though it may be a small percentage. If you invest $50,000 in an annuity that allows a 10 percent free withdrawal each year, and you withdraw $6,000, the penalty is only assessed on $1000 (which is the amount over the 10% free withdrawal of $5000).

The percentage of the penalty on the annuity may be higher than that charged as a penalty on a CD; however, if it is charged on a smaller percentage of the investment, the charge could be less. Here's an example: let's say you need $6,000 from your CD and you have a 1 percent penalty if you cash in your $50,000 CD early. The penalty amount would be $500 ($50,000 x 1 percent). In that same scenario, what would the penalty be for taking $6,000 from a $50,000 annuity that allows a 10 percent free withdrawal each year? If you are in a year in which 8 percent is the penalty for amounts over the free withdrawal, your penalty would be $80 ($1,000 x 8 percent).

That being said, annuities are long-term investments. If you have $100,000 and intend on putting the entire amount down on a house in two years, it would be foolish to invest in a ten-year annuity, then take it right back out after only two years and have to pay the penalty.

An annuity is an excellent choice for lifetime income. Which annuity is right for you and how much you invest will depend on a variety of issues, including age and risk tolerance. You should check with a qualified adviser to consider all of the options when choosing an annuity. Here are some questions for you to ask:

- How much is the free withdrawal each year? In other words, how much can you withdraw from the annuity without incurring a penalty?

- How long is the surrender period?

- What happens to the lump sum if there is money left in the account when you pass away? Does it go to your heirs?

- What are the fees and what do they cover?

In the past several years, bad advice from well-known radio or TV personalities has served to distort the truth about annuities and confuse consumers. Most of those giving the advice are not licensed financial professionals, have a very limited understanding of annuities and give advice on many different subjects, much of it having nothing to do with finances. But because the person is well known, has a platform and a following, consumers mistakenly consider their word the gospel.

Another problem with this type of information is that, typically, the person giving the advice does not go into specifics about what they are saying. For a person to say that all annuities are bad is like saying all cars are bad just because a few are lemons. You see my point. Does it make any sense at all to say that the only account for guaranteeing lifetime income is something you should avoid?

I have heard some popular media personalities advise people to only purchase a SPIA, which means the owner's beneficiaries will never be eligible to receive a lump sum payment from the funds that may be left in the annuity. This could be a substantial amount of money if the owner has received only a small portion of the account before the death of the insured. While a SPIA may be the perfect choice for some, to advise people that it is the only type of annuity that should be considered is absurd.

Annuities can be created with funds from many sources including checking accounts, savings accounts, brokerage accounts, employer plans and even other annuities, assuming replacement of the old annuity is deemed suitable. There are two tax qualifications for annuities: qualified and nonqualified.

A qualified annuity is normally funded with money that has not yet been taxed, such as an IRA, SEP, 403b, 401k, etc. Most employer plans will allow funds to be transferred out of the plan if a person is no longer employed there or they have reached the age of 59½. Many plans have become much more liberal in allowing portions of money to be transferred out before a person reaches 59½, a result of so many employees who were within a few years of retirement losing much of their retirement accounts due to the market decline during the recession. Even our government began recommending annuities for those close to retirement.

Some people mistakenly believe that moving a qualified account will cause it to become taxable. However, when the funds are moved properly from one account to another, it does not trigger a taxable event.

A nonqualified annuity is one that is initially funded from accounts that have already been taxed. As the money grows in the annuity, the growth is tax-deferred until the person takes the money out. We will discuss this further in chapter 9 when we address tax planning.

Money that has already been taxed can go into a nonqualified annuity. If a person wants to transfer funds into a new nonqualified annuity from an existing one, it can be done through a 1035 exchange. By using this process, the interest that the old nonqualified annuity has earned will not become taxable during the exchange, as long as the funds are transferred directly from one insurance company to another. The 1035 exchange is a provision for transferring funds from one insurance product to another without creating a taxable event, similar to the 1031 exchange for real estate purchases.

In some cases it would be more advantageous for a woman who has built up a large amount of cash value in a life insurance policy to use the 1035 exchange and transfer the cash value into an annuity that could be used for income. Exchanging (or replacing) insurance contracts is highly regulated by the states, as it should be. You should seek the advice of a trained financial professional before surrendering any insurance contracts.

Annuities play a very important part in providing lifetime income, especially as pensions are being replaced with employer plans and

Social Security is becoming more questionable with every passing year. Women who have not set up a plan for lifetime income could certainly find themselves running out of money before the end of their life.

Consider all of your income sources. Make sure you have a plan for a lifetime of secure income no matter what circumstances may occur. Many women never take the time to do proper income planning. When circumstances change and their income is reduced, many times it is at a difficult time such as the loss of a spouse. Trying to deal with financial matters at a time like that can be overwhelming, to say the least.

Proper income planning consists of deciding which one of the four quadrants is right for you to earn money, determining how much of your earnings you should set aside for future retirement income and making sure you have sufficient vehicles for providing guaranteed lifetime income once you retire.

CHAPTER SUMMARY

Three categories of income:

1) Temporary income: wages, loan repayments and spousal income

2) Variable income: return on investments, rental income and employment

3) Lifetime income: Social Security, pensions and annuities

Pension (SPIA) options:

1) Life Only: lifetime income payments for one person

2) Joint and Survivor: lifetime income payments for two people

3) Life with Period Certain: lifetime income payments for one person that will continue for a certain time period if that person dies before the time period ends

Annuities types:

1) Fixed Annuity: have a set amount of interest

2) Indexed Annuity: interest can be fixed or earned based on an index

3) Variable Annuity: mutual funds inside of an insurance contract

P.U.R.S.E.S.

Tax qualification of annuities:

1) Qualified: funded from accounts where taxes have not been paid yet

2) Nonqualified: base of investment has already been taxed

CHAPTER 9

Tax Planning

There are only two things certain in life: death and taxes. Have you ever wondered where that cliché originated? It might surprise you to learn that Benjamin Franklin actually coined the phrase in a letter in which he stated, "Our constitution is an actual operation and everything appears to promise it will last: but in this world nothing can be said to be certain but death and taxes." Over 200 years later, no one has found a way to keep from dying, and Benjamin Franklin and his friends would never have stood for the amount of taxes we pay.[1]

As I mentioned earlier, there are three key components to a financial plan: income planning, tax planning and estate planning. Let's take a look at how we can address the two certainties in Benjamin Franklin's great quote regarding death and taxes. In the next chapter, we will deal with the death part when we address estate planning. For now, let's talk about the taxes part.

Paying taxes is a very real part of life; however, paying unnecessary taxes is, well, unnecessary!

Tax planning is too often overlooked. As a result, thousands of dollars are unnecessarily paid in taxes and/or heavy taxation burdens are unintentionally placed on heirs. Tax planning can be one of the biggest

*Paying unnecessary taxes is,
well, unnecessary!*

difference makers in whether or not you will have a solid financial plan for yourself and those who will eventually inherit your estate. Many people spend their time and energy focused only on the performance of investments and completely overlook how lack of tax planning can negatively impact an overall portfolio, as well as what will be left to heirs. I call this the PUT Syndrome: Paying Unnecessary Taxes.

Over the next ten years, the U.S. government expects to pay out $45.7 trillion; however, it expects to bring in only $39 trillion. To make up this difference, the government will likely need to raise taxes on much of the population, cut spending and cut back on Medicare and Social Security.[2] Considering all of this, a person must seriously address the issue of taxes.

Understanding the tax code is next to impossible. Did you know that the federal tax code was 400 pages in 1913, but that number grew to 70,000 by 2010? To give you an idea of what that looks like, the Bible has about 700,000 words. The number of words in the federal tax code: 3,700,000.[3] Does this make you feel that tax planning would be far too complicated and therefore should be avoided? If so, you will be surprised to find that some simple steps can be taken to help eliminate unnecessary tax payments.

Americans hire over 1 million accountants every year to help with taxes and spend over $27.7 billion for tax-related services.[4] Finding out how much taxes you owe is extremely important, but finding out how much you *don't* owe can save you a bundle!

Taxes come in many forms: sales tax, property tax, income tax, capital gains tax and estate tax.

INCOME TAX

Many of these taxes are unavoidable. In this chapter, we will focus on the taxes that people most commonly overpay, beginning with income tax.

If you have ever held a job, you most likely paid some taxes on your income; however, wages are not the only things considered taxable. Other items that can fall into that category are interest and dividends on investments as well as Social Security benefits.

Depending on your income needs, you may be able to defer paying taxes on interest and dividends on your investments. This is another place where purchasing an annuity might make sense for you. We already know that your qualified investments, such as IRAs and employer plans, are considered tax-deferred. Putting these accounts in an annuity may be your smartest move for future income; however, since they are already tax-deferred, the annuity will not make a difference in their tax status.

Where an annuity can make a difference is with nonqualified accounts. Remember, these are the ones that have already had taxes paid on the base. If you have $100,000 in a nonqualified CD—meaning not an IRA CD or other qualified money—the interest you earn is not tax-deferred. Even though you may not be taking the interest and are just allowing it to roll back into your account, the interest is still reported on your income tax return. The same is true for other investment vehicles such as nonqualified mutual funds or stock dividends.

Reporting interest and dividends, which is not optional if these are nonqualified accounts, can potentially cause you to pay more income taxes in more than one way. First, they have the potential for pushing you into a higher tax bracket. Secondly, if you are collecting Social Security they can cause it to be taxed. Social Security is taxed according to income and marital status. When your income is higher, this can cause a direct effect on Social Security taxation, potentially causing up to 85 percent of Social Security benefits to be taxed.

For these reasons, many people consider a tax-deferred vehicle for their money. When these funds are put into a nonqualified annuity, the earnings become tax-deferred and are, therefore, not taxed until the money is actually taken out. In essence, a nonqualified annuity can be an excellent place for gaining some control over your tax bill.

CAPITAL GAINS TAX

Next, let's consider taxes on capital gains. These are taxes based on the profit made from the sale of an asset. The value of your assets can go up and down. As long as you do not sell them, the gain (or loss) will remain unrealized and is therefore not reported on your tax return.

In determining taxes on capital gains, there are two things to consider: how long you have owned the asset and the cost basis of the investment, which is the original value of the asset when you took ownership. One huge tax mistake can occur when a person makes someone an owner of an asset that is intended not to be theirs until the person passes away.

Here is an example: Let's just say that you own a stock portfolio that is worth $100,000. Your intention for this account is to pass it on to your son when you pass away. Thinking that if his name was put on the account as a joint owner, the account would pass more easily to him at your death, you add his name to the account. While this could potentially make passing the asset a simpler process at your death, it could also cause your son to pay unnecessary capital gain taxes.

If the stock portfolio was worth $100,000 when you added your son as an owner, but it had grown to $300,000 by the time you died, and your son sells the stock at $300,000, he would potentially owe capital gains taxes on his portion of the $200,000 gain: the difference between the value of the stock when he became an owner and when he sold it. If he had not been added to the account as an owner and instead had inherited the $300,000 at your death, he could have sold it for the value of $300,000 and owed no capital gains as a result of the sale. He would have gotten a step up in basis, meaning that his base was $300,000 when he inherited it.

This is a very basic example. Because taxes are complicated and have a lot of moving parts, you should check with your CPA on all tax questions you may have. However, knowing the basics can help you know the right questions to ask and could potentially help your heirs avoid unnecessary taxes.

ESTATE TAX

The last tax we will address over which people make avoidable mistakes is in dealing with estate taxes. These can be imposed when a taxable estate is transferred to beneficiaries at someone's death. What portion of the estate is considered taxable? As far as federal estate taxes go, anything that exceeds the federal estate tax exemption, which at the time of this writing is $5,340,000 for individuals ($10,680,000 for a married couple). For many, this is not an issue to be concerned with; however, the heirs of wealthy individuals pay thousands, tens of thousands and even hundreds of thousands of dollars in estate taxes, many times unnecessarily because of inadequate estate planning.

Every person is entitled to the $5,340,000 gift or estate tax exemption; this value can be passed on while a person is living or after their death. Even if your estate is nowhere near that amount, many people still get confused by the issue of gift tax and tax exclusions. A person may give another person something of value during their lifetime. As long as the value of the gift does not exceed the *annual exclusion*—$14,000 in 2014—this will not count toward their *lifetime exemption* of $5,340,000. The portion of a gift that exceeds the exclusion in any one year to the same person will count toward their lifetime exemption. Many times people are under the misconception that if they give a person more than $14,000 in a given year, the gift will incur a gift tax. That is incorrect. As long as a person has not given away more than their lifetime exemption, a gift tax will not be due.

An estate over the exemption will incur estate taxes. Many people immediately dismiss this subject due to the fact that their estate is under the exempted amount; however, you should be aware of what is considered when placing a value on an estate, which is basically everything you may own: real estate, businesses, accounts (including retirement accounts), personal property and life insurance. A person who has valued their estate at $4,500,000 but left out a $2,000,000 life insurance policy may mistakenly ignore estate planning, thinking they are under the exemption. Make sure you have included *all* assets when determining whether estate taxes should be considered as a part of your overall estate plan.

TAX PENALTIES

Now let's move on to another area where people pay the IRS unnecessarily: tax penalties. While most people are aware of common penalties such as underpayment of estimated taxes or not filing your taxes on time, there are other penalties that are overlooked. These penalties involve those associated with qualified accounts such as IRAs.

If you take money out of a qualified account before you reach the age of 59½, the IRS will penalize you. The penalty amount is 10 percent of the withdrawal. There is an exception to this known as the 72T rule; however, there are very specific guidelines that must be followed in this special allowance. Make sure you speak to a qualified financial professional if you are considering this. Exemptions from tax penalties are also available in certain hardship situations. Again, be very clear on this subject before taking early withdrawals from a qualified account.

Not only are there penalties for taking early withdrawals on qualified accounts, there are penalties for taking late withdrawals as well. When a person turns 70½, an RMD (Required Minimum Distribution) must be taken in order to avoid a *50% taxation penalty!* At some point, the IRS wants taxes to be paid on funds that have been tax-deferred. When a person turns 70½, it is required that they take their first distribution no later than April 1 of the year following the one in which they reached age 70½. If you decide to wait until April 1 to take your first RMD, don't forget that another distribution will be required by December 31 of that year, as well as all subsequent years.

Many people are unaware that an RMD is also required when a person inherits a qualified account such as an IRA. The same 50 percent penalty is applied for failing to take the distribution on time.

Knowing the few simple facts that have been discussed in this chapter can potentially help you save thousands of dollars on taxes during your lifetime, as well as what you will ultimately pass on to your heirs. In the next chapter, we will discuss more ways to maximize inheritances through proper estate planning.

CHAPTER SUMMARY

Types of Taxes:

- Sales Tax—Goods and Services

- Property Tax—Real Estate

- Income Tax—Wages, Interest, Dividends, Social Security

- Capital Gaines Tax—profit from the sale of an asset

- Estate Tax—due on an estate after a person dies

Avoiding Unnecessary Taxes:

- Using tax-deferred accounts

- Avoiding capital gains through step-up provision

Tax Penalties:

- Underpaying taxes

- Paying taxes late

- Premature withdrawals from a qualified account

- Failing to take a Required Minimum Distribution

CHAPTER 10

Estate Planning

As you may recall in chapter 2, one shocking statistic is the fact that by the year 2050, $41 trillion will transfer to the next generation, but much of it will never make it to the intended heirs. Much of this is due to the lack of good estate planning. If you prefer passing your assets onto your loved ones instead of people you have never met, estate planning is a must. For people who are too busy or too apathetic to pursue a good estate plan, enormous amounts of their estates could potentially be paid in taxes and/or legal fees, instead of being handed down to the intended recipients.

Not only is estate planning essential in making sure heirs receive maximum assets but it can also save years of hassle, complication and stress while settling an estate.

Many women do not feel the need for estate planning because they do not believe they have enough assets to be considered an *estate*. On the contrary, if you have possessions no matter how big or small, you have an estate!

If you don't care what happens to those possessions once you pass away, then estate planning may not be a top priority for you; however, I find that most women want to make sure the things they spent their lives acquiring get into the hands of the people and/or charities they love.

Legal documents play an important role in proper estate planning.

As I have said, the term *estate planning* may seem daunting to some. And while it may be true that having a large estate might require more sophisticated planning, there are certain documents and procedures every woman should consider for maximizing the efficiency of transferring assets at death. In addition, proper legal documents can make life easier for a person *before* she passes away.

LEGAL DOCUMENTS FOR SETTLING ESTATES

Two of the most common legal documents used for passing on assets to heirs are a Last Will and Testament, which I will refer to simply as a will, and a Revocable Living Trust.

While a will is a legal document, many people do not understand how it actually works. My best definition of a will is a legal document that lists your desires and requests for how you want your estate to be settled. A will goes through probate, a process for proving the authenticity of the document that helps with the transfer of ownership for the assets of the deceased person. However, what most people fail to understand is that having a will does not guarantee that assets will be distributed as you have requested. During the probate process, anyone can contest your will if that person has just cause. If your will is contested, the settling of your estate could drag on for months and even years. This can cause a serious drain on the assets, which are used to pay legal fees, not to mention the time spent and aggravation experienced by those who are trying to settle the estate.

Revocable Living Trusts are becoming increasingly popular. Although once used mostly to settle large estates, they are being used more and more often to settle even modest estates. One of the main reasons for this is the ability to avoid probate. If a trust has been funded properly, it is the owner of the person's assets; when the trustor passes away, the assets are still owned by the trust, and the power has already been given to a trustee or successor trustee to settle the estate without the involvement of probate.

There are additional benefits for choosing a Revocable Living Trust. First, since it eliminates the necessity of probate, it can keep the settling of an estate from becoming public record. Many people want the privacy provided through the use of this legal instrument.

Another benefit in owning a Revocable Living Trust is that it can eliminate the need for joint ownership with children. One of the biggest mistakes made by women is adding their children's names to their accounts and properties. You may be putting your assets at serious risk by adding someone's name as a joint owner. If a person whom you have named as a joint owner of your assets is sued, your assets can be lost. What a horrible thing! In addition to this potential disaster is the loss of the step-up provision we discussed in chapter 9 in regard to capital gains. Please reconsider putting your children's names on your assets. The reason most people add their children's names on their accounts and properties is to eliminate probate. With a properly funded Revocable Living Trust in place, you can achieve the same result without putting your assets at risk or causing your heirs unnecessary taxes.

You should check with an attorney to find out which legal document best suits your needs. But consider these two things when choosing an attorney. First, make sure the attorney fully understands estate planning documents and how they work. Many people arbitrarily choose any attorney merely because that person is an attorney. Maybe it is someone you used in the past to draw up legal documents for property purchases, to settle a divorce or is simply a friend of the family. While that attorney may have the necessary estate planning skills, don't automatically assume that is the case. You want to make sure you are dealing with an estate planning expert. Just as you would not go to a podiatrist for brain surgery, you should choose legal professionals who are specialists in their fields. Secondly, make sure the advice you are receiving from the attorney is in your best interest. Unfortunately, some people have been misled by attorneys who were more eager to probate a will than draw up the legal documents most advantageous for the client and their heirs.

My husband and I have chosen a Revocable Living Trust for our estate. Knowing all of the possible pitfalls of just having a will, we decided that we are much more comfortable with the trust. Again, each person should decide for themselves which is best for them. Discussing your goals and desires with an attorney who understands estate planning will help determine what the best steps are for achieving those goals.

There are other ways of passing assets directly to heirs. If you have a life insurance or annuity contract, you can pass them on through beneficiary designation. This holds true for qualified accounts including IRAs and employer plans like 401ks.

With most bank and brokerage accounts that are not qualified, you can simply have a POD (Payable On Death) or TOD (Transfer On Death) added to the account. Upon your death, the account will pass directly to your beneficiaries. However, beware of serious consequences for setting things up incorrectly. Some women tell me they have listed only one of their children's names as a beneficiary of an account because that child knows to divide the account up between all of her children. Even if you trust one of your children to be fair and to handle things according to your wishes, this is not a good idea. You can potentially cause that one child to owe a huge tax bill that he or she alone will be responsible for. Another issue with setting up accounts with a POD or TOD is that contingencies are usually not allowed, potentially forfeiting the opportunity to pass assets on down the bloodline.

OTHER IMPORTANT LEGAL DOCUMENTS

A Durable Power of Attorney for Asset Management is used to give another person the authority to make financial decisions for someone, usually in the case of incapacitation but not always. I feel that this is one of the most important legal documents a woman needs to have in place during her lifetime. (Note: When a person dies, this document ceases to be in effect.) If a person becomes incapacitated and has not named someone to serve in this role, the court may appoint a stranger to fill this position.

Someone who is a joint owner of an account (or other asset) can usually handle the financial matters of the account unless the account requires both signatures. This would be true in the case of a husband and wife being joint owners of a checking or brokerage account. But even married couples cannot be joint owners of a qualified account such as an IRA, 401k or 403b. Many married people forget this fact and find that they have no power to act on behalf of their spouse with regard to their qualified accounts. This can be devastating in certain circumstances. For instance, if a wife needs funds from her husband's retirement account while he is incapacitated in order to pay the bills, her hands are tied if she does not have the proper legal document in place (in this case, a Durable Power of Attorney for Asset Management).

There are several different types of Power of Attorney documents. Some allow only for a single transaction, while others are more comprehensive. Make sure you have the correct document.

A Power of Attorney for Health Care Management works much like the Durable Power of Attorney for Asset Management, but it gives authority for someone to make medical decisions rather than financial ones for an individual.

A Pour-over Will is normally included when setting up a trust. The function of this document is to make sure that if any asset is left out of the trust, it is eventually poured back into the trust. Although this provision works for getting the asset into the trust, it does not keep the asset from going through probate. Therefore, the time and expense of probate can be incurred before the asset gets into the trust.

The purpose of a Living Will is primarily to give instructions to relatives or physicians on how medical treatment and life-support issues should be handled when a person is facing death. Having this document in order can take a tremendous burden off family members.

Legal documents play a huge role in proper estate planning. Many people wait too long to begin the process. On more occasions than I like to remember, I have seen people rush to try to get documents drawn up when a person is near death but it was too late. Either the person died before the documents were signed or they were debilitated to the point that signing them was impossible. Even if a person can sign documents physically, they must do so while having a sound mind.

Don't delay in taking care of such important affairs. What I said in chapter 7 bears repeating here: taking a little time to deal with these matters can save you and your heirs what is sometimes enormous amounts of loss, worry, grief and stress. Don't leave yourself or your family without options.

TAXATION OF INHERITANCES

As you draw up your estate plan, you must think about the tax consequences of the assets you are passing on to your heirs. Which assets you pass and how they are received can determine the income-tax liability for the recipient.

Let's begin with life insurance. Did you know that the death benefit from a life insurance policy usually passes income tax free? For this reason, if you are planning to leave an IRA account to your children and a life insurance death benefit to a charity, you might want to reverse that decision. By leaving the IRA to the charity (assuming it is set up properly as a nonprofit organization), there will be no taxes due. Making the children the beneficiaries of the life insurance will not cause them to pay taxes. Make sense?

Life insurance can be an extremely important part of your estate plan, not only from an income tax standpoint but by maximizing what your heirs will receive. Do you realize that your health is a very important asset? As strange as it may sound, being healthy during your lifetime can maximize your estate at your death. If you are insurable and have money that is intended for heirs, you can pay life insurance premiums with that money while you are living and potentially leave your heirs twice or three times as much as they would have received without the life insurance in place.

Let's assume you have $300,000 of nonqualified money you plan on passing to your heirs, and you feel you most likely will not need the funds during your lifetime. Depending on your age and insurability, you could purchase a life insurance policy that could potentially result in passing $600,000 or even $1 million to your heirs income tax free. Another way people sometimes fund a life insurance policy is with the Required Minimum Distribution they are forced to take. Instead of a one-time dump in, like in the first example, they pay annual premiums that come from the RMD.

Next let's discuss passing IRAs at death. A spouse of a deceased individual has a provision for inheriting such accounts that others do not. This is called a spousal assumption. As the words indicate, the spouse can assume the account and have it become his or her IRA. Or a spouse can inherit the IRA the same way children or other beneficiaries would. When an IRA is passed on at death, an RMD will need to begin at some point, the timing of which will be based on how the IRA was passed: spousal assumption or inheritance. Either way, it is imperative for this distribution to take place at the proper time. As you will recall from chapter 9, the penalty for not taking an RMD is 50 percent taxation.

Another important factor to consider for someone inheriting an IRA is how funds will be distributed to them. An inherited IRA that is paid out to an individual becomes taxable immediately. If a person does not want to take the IRA in a lump sum but wants to move the account to a different institution, they may do so by setting up an Inherited IRA account and having the funds sent directly from the old institution to the one where the new account has been set up.

Whether the inherited IRA remains in the same institution or is transferred to a new place, the RMD is still required. The amount of the RMD will depend on the age of the person who inherited it. Required minimum distributions are calculated based on the individual's life expectancy. If a twenty-year-old inherits an IRA of $100,000, the RMD amount will be less than that of a forty-year-old because there are more years in which to stretch out the distribution. This concept is called a Stretch IRA: stretching the distribution out over a lifetime.

In the past, before the implementation of the Stretch IRA rules, a person only had five years in which to have the account fully distributed, which sometimes led to a major tax liability.

Understanding how to properly inherit an IRA can save the recipient what can sometimes be thousands of dollars in taxes. Unfortunately, due to lack of information, a person who receives an IRA can wind up taking the money in a lump sum and ultimately owing a huge amount in taxes. If the person spends all of the money, then learns of the tax liability, this can be financially devastating.

Make sure you and you loved ones are informed about IRA inheritances. Seek advice from a qualified financial professional such as your CPA.

Let me quickly discuss one final thing regarding inheritances. Over the years, some women have told me that when they receive an inheritance from their parents, they want to make sure that if there is any portion of it left when they pass away, it go to their children, not to their husband (or his new wife and her children).

While marital asset laws vary greatly among states, one thing to remember if you want to pass an inheritance down your bloodline is to keep the money, or other asset, in your name only. If the funds are ever comingled—in a checking account, for instance—this makes for a much more vulnerable situation in which to meet your goals.

As you can see, there are many things to consider in putting together a proper estate plan. You will most likely need qualified individuals to help you sort through each piece, which may include a financial adviser, a CPA, an attorney or any combination of these. Do not take advice from individuals who are not qualified to answer your questions.

CHAPTER SUMMARY

Basic Estate Planning Documents:

- Last Will and Testament

- Revocable Living Trust

- Durable Power of Attorney for Asset Management

- Power of Attorney for Health Care

- Pour-over Will

- Living Will

Taxation of Assets

- Life insurance passes income tax free

- Spousal assumption of IRAs

- Inherited IRAs

- Stretch IRAs

- Required Minimum Distribution

PART III

An Action Plan

CHAPTER 11

Three Steps For Change

After reading the first two sections of this book, do you feel there are areas where changes are needed in your overall financial plan? Have you been guilty of believing some of the money myths that were discussed in chapter 4 or making mistakes mentioned in chapter 6? If not, congratulations! You probably fall within one-quarter percent of all women in the world. Most of us, at some point in our lives, have been guilty of stinking thinking by believing myths about money that simply aren't true, or we have made mistakes along the way. Normally, there are at least a few areas of a financial plan that need to be changed or improved upon.

Change is not easy for most people. In his book *Dream Giver*, Bruce Wilkinson tells a compelling story of a person who lived in the land of Familiar. He knew there was something better waiting for him, but it would require taking bold steps.[1]

A woman can change almost any area in her life for the better; however, change takes both courage and effort. The definition of effort is to use physical or mental energy to do something; an exertion of strength or will; an earnest attempt.

Change takes both
courage and effort.

Sometimes change can make you feel uncomfortable. Unfortunately, there are scores of women who make poor choices and stay in a bad situation simply because it is familiar. However, there are many ladies who are proactive and understand the rewards that come from making the effort to change their situation for the better. Since you are reading this book, I would say you probably fit in the latter group.

A person can change practically any situation in her life by following these three steps:

STEP #1 – CONNECT WITH THE TRUTH

While this may sound relatively easy, many times it can be the hardest of the three. Digging deep and being honest with yourself about your situation can sometimes be painful. However, a woman must not be afraid to evaluate herself if she is serious about making changes.

With that said, read over the following comments and put a checkmark in front of the ones that are true for you. Remember to be honest. No one but you needs to see your answers. If you are planning to give this book to someone else and don't want them to see your answers, use a pencil so your answers can be erased when you are finished, or write your answers on a separate sheet of paper. Either way, this will be a good exercise for connecting with the truth.

We will begin with the money myths listed in chapter 4. If you are guilty of believing any of these myths—at least before you read this book—don't be afraid to put a checkmark in front of the one(s) that apply to you. If you're not sure about one, it is OK to put a question mark instead of a checkmark. There will be no tallying of a score. This is just to help you focus on areas that need to change.

Again, be honest. If you are not honest, you will be wasting your time doing the exercise. Dig deep and search for your truest feelings.

Check the money myths that you have been guilty of believing at some point in your life:

_____ *I would be showing disrespect to my husband if I tried to be more involved with our finances.*

_____ *I don't have to concern myself with money issues because I can rely on a man.*

_____ *I don't have to concern myself with money issues because I plan to inherit plenty from my family.*

_____ *I am secure with the company I work for.*

_____ *I can depend on the government to take care of me.*

_____ *Women aren't supposed to understand money matters.*

_____ *The more money a person has, the more materialistic she is.*

_____ *Money causes a person to be proud.*

_____ *Rich people are greedy.*

_____ *The Bible says money is the root of evil.*

Now, let's move on to the mistakes that were listed in chapter 6. If you have been guilty of any of these mistakes, place a checkmark in front of that statement.

_____ *I spend little or no time planning for my financial future.*

_____ *I am uninformed or misinformed about my family finances.*

_____ *I think money isn't that important as long as you have love.*

_____ *My investments and spending habits are not aligned with my goals and dreams.*

_____ *I make emotional decisions about money instead of logical ones.*

_____ *I live in financial la-la land.*

_____ *I do not have a basic understanding of money, investments and asset protection.*

_____ *I am potentially putting heavy burdens on my children in the areas of taxation, long-term care and settling my estate.*

_____ *I don't believe that my estate is large enough for an estate plan.*

_____ *I potentially have unsuitable insurance policies.*

_____ *I tend to trip over a hundred-dollar bill to pick up a nickel.*

_____ *I am a procrastinator.*

_____ *I tend to believe that life will always look the way it does today.*

_____ *I have a portfolio that does not fit and is not age-appropriate for me.*

_____ *I have a portfolio that is too complicated.*

_____ *I am disorganized.*

_____ *I don't maximize income opportunities.*

_____ *I seek advice from unqualified people.*

_____ *I probably overpay taxes.*

_____ *I take unnecessary risks.*

_____ *I am failing to protect myself and my family from catastrophic events.*

_____ *I spend money I don't have to buy things I don't need to impress people I don't like.*

As I said, connecting with the truth is not easy. For sure, there will be some ladies who are guilty of statements they skipped over or did not check, not because they don't want others to see what they marked but because it is too hard for them to admit it to themselves. If you put a question mark in any of the spaces, now would be a good time to go back through your answers to determine whether that question mark should be changed to a checkmark.

I realize this exercise can be unpleasant, but think about it like this: A person who knows she has a health issue because she is not feeling well will most likely make a visit to the doctor to determine what the problem is. This is a necessary prerequisite to having the doctor plan out a course of action for healing. Can you imagine walking into the doctor's office and having him/her prescribe medications or determining you need surgery without that person asking you any questions or doing a physical examination? That would be ludicrous!

In the same way, you must determine where the problems are before designing a financial plan. Just as catastrophic health issues or death can sometimes be prevented, so can financial disasters. A woman who has just been told by her physician that she has breast cancer has a very difficult time connecting with that truth, but so many lives have been saved as a result of detecting the problem before it was too late and beginning the proper treatment.

A woman who will boldly connect with the truth about her financial situation will be in a position to make good decisions regarding what must be done to secure her financial future.

STEP #2 – TAKE RESPONSIBILITY

Finding someone else to blame for problems is normally our first reaction when we connect with the truth and are brought face-to-face with harsh realities. As humans, we don't like the pressure of taking responsibility; putting it on someone else's shoulders can relieve us of the guilt. While it may be true that someone else is the cause—or at least partly the cause—for your being in the bad financial situation you may be in, the blame game does nothing to put you any closer to a solution to the problem. As a matter of fact, it may cause you to experience stress or depression and sap you of the energy needed to get yourself in a better position.

Some women are certainly in financial predicaments caused by circumstances beyond their control, such as the loss of a spouse through divorce or death. But staying in a place of grief too long can turn into depression, bitterness or even hostility, which does nothing to improve your situation. Take the proper amount of time to deal with your emotions, but, at some point, move on to a better place mentally, emotionally and financially.

Now that we have acknowledged that some problems are the result of someone else's actions, let's begin to deal with ourselves. Too many women avoid taking responsibility by constantly making excuses:

1) "I don't have time to deal with my finances or get my estate plan done"
2) "I don't make enough money"
3) "I don't know who to trust"
4) "I don't know where to start"
5) "It's too late" etc.

Might I make a suggestion? Write all of your excuses down on a piece of paper; then set it on fire! Excuses are going to do nothing to get you closer to your financial goals. Let them go; they have no value at all. Woulda, coulda, shoulda will get you nowhere. Stop making excuses, stop blaming and for goodness' sake, stop whining!

Even if you have had bad things happen to you, most times you can move past them and improve your situation. Lou Holtz once said, "Life is ten percent what happens to you and ninety percent how you respond to it."[2]

One final thought on what causes women not to take responsibility: they rely too much on other people, or even one person. Often they sit idly by, thinking that someone else is steering the ship, when suddenly there is a crash. Loads of women suffered from this disaster during the market decline of 2008. I have spoken to many women who tell me that they don't know what they would do if something happened to their financial adviser because they have no clue what is going on with their own portfolio. Yikes!

Having financial professionals to help guide you with decision making is necessary most of the time, but no one will ever care more about your money than you. Handing your portfolio over to an adviser and never asking questions or having a review is simply not a good idea.

STEP #3 – TAKE ACTION

The old cliché "Talk is cheap" cannot be more true than in regard to financial planning. Some women spend years talking about how they need to get their financial and estate plan in order. Did I say years? Yes, years. If they would have only spent a tenth or less of the time they used up in talking about it actually doing it, their financial and estate plan would most likely be complete and solid as a rock.

I have held meetings with women—and men—who admit that getting this important work done is a must. At the moment they feel a sense of urgency. But as they go back to their busy lives, that sense of urgency grows dim and eventually disappears from sight. Sometimes taking time to get a financial and estate plan gets crowded out by very important things like planning a vacation, playing golf or watching TV. Of course I am being fictitious and somewhat sarcastic, but I am also being truthful. This actually happens. Has it happened to you?

If you have not taken the time to do proper planning, let me encourage you to take steps to do so now. Action steps are empowering; they create momentum. You will be amazed at how fast your plan will begin to come together once you start to move in that direction. Do something every day, even if it is small, toward developing your plan. Small steps lead to big victories.

Stop worrying about the things you can't do anything about and start taking steps toward changing the things you can. Remember, whatever direction you go, make sure it is forward. Before you know it, you will have a strong plan that will not crash and burn when life happens. You will have a solid anchor that will hold your financial portfolio in place when the storms come—and, most likely, they *will* come at some point, to some degree. Be ready. Don't be caught off guard.

CHAPTER SUMMARY

Three Steps for Change:

1) Connect with the Truth

   • Be honest and real

   • Don't be afraid to evaluate yourself

   • Dig deep

2) Take Responsibility

   • Stop blaming

   • Stop making excuses

   • Stop whining

   • Stop relying so heavily on others

3) Take Action

   • Talk is cheap

   • Take the first step; actions steps are empowering

   • Small steps lead to big victories

CHAPTER 12

Portfolio Blueprint

A blueprint, simply put, is a detailed outline or plan of action; it serves as a guide for constructing things. Building a customized financial plan that meets your financial goals will require a blueprint that you can follow to completion.

Allow me to digress and say you should not be discouraged if you completed the exercise in the last chapter to find that you have already made many mistakes. As mentioned in chapter 6, if mistakes have already caused damage to your financial situation, you need to assess the damage, take inventory of what is left and then reevaluate and redesign your plan.

My intention for being rather blunt throughout much of this book has not been to make you feel bad but rather to help you get a realistic picture of finances and what it takes to become financially secure. By understanding statistics and recognizing mistakes, you will have concrete information that will serve as a strong foundation for building your plan.

No matter what your mistakes (or misfortunes) have been, everyone has a starting point. For some the journey may be a little longer than for others, but everyone can get herself to a better place if she is

Not having the right vehicles to get you where you want to go will most likely leave you stranded in a place that was not your intended destination.

willing to put forth the effort to do so. In order to reach your ultimate destination, you must determine your starting point (Point A), decide where you want to end up (Point B) and then design a plan that will get you there.

Determine what your Point A is by looking at your current situation. Write down all of your assets. You will want to include things like your home and other real estate, your business, personal property like cars, furniture, etc. and bank accounts, brokerage accounts, retirement accounts and insurance policies; basically, all of your possessions. Then consider your liabilities: the mortgage on a home, student loans, business loans, credit card debt, etc. Next think about your current income; the amount as well as the source.

Once you have finished listing your current situation, you will have established your Point A. Now you will want to determine your point B. These are your goals. Be realistic, but do not sell yourself short. Remember the Henry Ford quote mentioned earlier in this book: "Whether you think you can, or you think you can't—you're right."

Goals come in two categories: short-term and long-term. A short-term goal may include getting a better-paying job or eliminating small debts. Long-term goals could mean paying off your mortgage or creating a nest egg. If you are already retired, your goals may consist of protecting your current assets and securing lifetime income.

Whatever your goals are, you will need financial vehicles to reach them. These accounts and investments will be the tools that will help you build a sound financial plan.

As you will recall, the R in the acronym, "P.U.R.S.E.S." stands for Resources Available. To design the plan that is right for you, I am going to describe the basic resources I mentioned in chapter 1. You will need to decide which of these tools are needed in your tool box for building your customized plan.

BANK ACCOUNTS

Checking. This is normally the first type of bank account most people own. The main purpose is to have money go in and out as necessary. Deposits are made from any number of sources. Then payments are made from the account, either through checks, debit cards or ETF (Electronic Transfer of Funds). A checking account is pretty basic. Banks normally do not pay much interest on them (if any at all) because it is considered a very short-term account with no restrictions on transactions. Some banks charge a fee for this service.

Savings. Many people establish a savings account as a holding tank for money they don't intend to spend right away but want to have accessibility to with no restrictions. Interest earned is normally not much higher than that on a checking account.

Money Markets. This works very much like a savings account. However, money markets are normally more restrictive on numbers of transactions allowed; therefore, they may pay a little more interest than that on a savings account.

Certificates of Deposit. CDs tend to be the most restrictive of bank accounts; however, the interest they earn will usually be higher than other accounts offered by banks. Interest is based on economic factors as well as the length of the term for which a CD was purchased. Normally, the longer the term, the better the interest will be. Penalties are a common part of a CD if cashed in before the term has expired.

These bank accounts are considered fairly safe. The FDIC (Federal Deposit Insurance Corporation) insures the accounts; however, coverage amounts can change. Staying informed on amounts of coverage is very important. The FDIC's ability to pay has been a topic of concern by some as confidence wanes in regard to the strength of the U.S. economy. With that said, many people still feel comfortable with FDIC coverage.

BROKERAGE ACCOUNTS

Most people use brokerage accounts for investing in vehicles such as stocks, bonds and mutual funds. Investment choices seem endless; however, two important factors that should be considered by the investor are risk tolerance and age.

For a person who is adverse to loss, risky investments that go up and down with the market can be maddening. A person who is retired and heavily dependent on investments for income also needs to weigh out the risk factor. A younger person who has many years to recover market losses before needing the money is in a far different situation than that of an older person who may not have time to recoup any losses she may experience.

A good financial adviser who helps with picking your investments should be keenly aware of your risk tolerance, goals and time horizon.

Investments such as stocks and bonds can be held directly by the investor rather than using a brokerage firm. Some people prefer to handle their own investments, while others would rather pay for the services of a licensed broker.

Whether a person decides to invest on her own or use a financial professional, investing in any vehicle that can potentially lose value is something that should be done with caution. The market can be like some friends: really good to you for a very long time but then turn on you without much warning. An investor needs to know how deep the relationship needs to be with the market and when it is time to get out.

INSURANCE

The purchasing of insurance should be determined by what type of protection is needed in your overall financial and estate plan.

Life Insurance. This product is an important consideration at any age. For a young family with the responsibility of raising small children, life insurance can play a huge part in the financial stability if a parent passes away. For an older person who needs income, the death benefit can replace the loss of spousal income. And the cash value of a life insurance policy can be put into an annuity for income through a 1035 exchange.

Other reasons for having life insurance range all the way from covering burial expenses to paying federal estate taxes. The death benefit from a life insurance policy is usually income tax free. A more sophisticated use can be funding an ILIT (Irrevocable Life Insurance Trust), which allows the life insurance to be placed outside of an estate, thereby avoiding potential estate taxes.

For a person who has money that is intended for her heirs, life insurance can greatly enhance the amount the beneficiary will receive.

Business owners may take out a life insurance policy on a key employee to cover expenses incurred by the company should that employee pass away. Some use life insurance to fund a Buy/Sell Agreement, which allows for a deceased person's interest in the business to be sold to a partner with the death benefit.

Remember, health is an asset. If an insurance company has reason to believe the insurance is needed and the person seeking the insurance is insurable, it will make an offering to the individual, letting her know what the cost of the policy will be. Based on the premiums and the amount of life insurance offered, a person can decide if she is comfortable with the terms of the contract.

As you can see, life insurance can be useful in all three elements of a plan: income planning, tax planning and estate planning.

Annuities. An annuity is an insurance product and also covers many areas of planning. Annuities are the only financial vehicles that can ensure lifetime income. An excellent place for qualified money, people love annuities for rolling their IRAs, 401ks, and other retirement accounts into, which can create an income for the rest of their life.

From a tax-planning standpoint, many people use annuities to help defer taxes on nonqualified accounts. The earnings do not become taxable until they are distributed, thus giving people more control over when they want to pay taxes on the earnings.

Sometimes people place money into an annuity and begin lifetime payments that fund the premiums for a life insurance policy. If set up properly, not only does the beneficiary receive the death benefit from the life insurance policy but also any funds that may still be left in the annuity policy.

Annuities are long-term products. When considering adding an annuity to your portfolio, determine how long you want to keep it, what purpose(s) it will serve and the terms and conditions of the contract.

Life insurance and annuities should be reviewed to make sure the beneficiaries are correct on them. I'm always amazed when I ask a client who the beneficiary is on their insurance policies because, believe it or not, most of the time they are not 100 percent sure. Beneficiaries can be updated easily by contacting your insurance company.

Long-Term Care Insurance. With people living longer and the cost of medical care constantly increasing, long-term care insurance may need to be considered. The premiums for this type of coverage will depend on your age, your health and how much coverage you desire.

As the statistics revealed, a large portion of the population will need long-term care at some point. Many people are in a position to self-insure, meaning they have the necessary funds to pay for the care themselves. For those who do not, long-term care insurance may be their best option. Even for people who could afford to pay themselves but prefer to pass assets on to their children, purchasing a long-term care policy might serve them well.

Growing old is not the only reason for needing long-term care. A person suffering from a stroke, Alzheimer's or an accident at any age may need an extended period of care.

For a person who has been funding a life insurance policy they may no longer need, paying premiums for a long-term care policy could make more sense.

OTHER INVESTMENTS

In addition to the various accounts, investments and products just described, there are many other opportunities for investments, such as real estate or even a business. Evaluate each one of your choices; then pick the ones that are right for you. Which ones are a good fit for helping you reach your goals?

Not having the right vehicles to get you where you want to go will most likely leave you stranded in a place that was not your intended destination.

Remember what the P in P.U.R.S.E.S. stands for: Purpose Based Planning. Taking inventory of your income, assets and liabilities, determining your needs and goals, then choosing the proper tools to build your plan will result in a customized, Purpose Based Plan for you.

Chances are that you will need the assistance of a financial professional for picking the right investments and deciding what type of life insurance and annuity policies might be best. But having a clear understanding of where you currently are and where you ultimately want to go will serve you well in communicating with your adviser. Can you imagine getting in a cab and expecting the cab driver to know what direction to take you if you don't know where you are going?

As you go through life, you will need to make adjustments to your plan along the way. When a ship begins a journey toward a predetermined destination and unexpected winds come up, the sail must be adjusted to keep the ship on course. The same principle is true for a financial plan. Being just a few degrees off course over a period of time can take you far from your intended destination.

If you have gotten off course through wrong thinking, mistakes or misfortune, now is the time to alter your course and get back on track.

Make sure your financial plan is designed to help you meet your goals and has the characteristics of a strong plan described in chapter 7.

When designing your plan, you will want to remember the first four D words described in chapter 3:

Dream: Take time to think about what you really want. Are you happy with your current job, or is there something out there you would enjoy doing more or would provide a better income?

Destination: Where do you want to go? What are your goals?

Decision: Make decisions that will help you achieve financial success and security. Which investment choices are the right vehicles for taking you where you want to go?

Detox: Get rid of anything holding you back. It is time to move forward and put yourself and your family in the best financial situation possible.

Once you design your plan, you will be able to visualize what can be built from your portfolio blueprint!

CHAPTER SUMMARY

1) Determine your Point A: where you currently are

2) Decide on your Point B: where do you want to end up

3) Choose the right tools to build your plan

- Bank Accounts: checking, savings, money markets, CDs

- Brokerage Accounts: stocks, bonds, mutual funds

- Insurance: life insurance, annuities, long-term care

- Other Investments: real estate, business

CHAPTER 13

Implementing Your Plan

In chapter 12 we reviewed the first four D words in designing your plan: Dream, Destination, Decision and Detox. Now let's quickly take a look at the last four:

Do List: Making a do list will be imperative in implementing your plan. As we move through this chapter, you will need to make a list of all the things that need to be done in order to reach your desired goals.

Discipline: Once you get started, you must be disciplined to stick to your plan. Distractions will surely come your way. However, you must focus on your do list until it is completed.

Determination: Obstacles will pop up, and there may be days when you want to procrastinate or even quit. But you must keep moving forward to fully implement your plan.

Deadline: Remember, a goal without a deadline is just a dream. Having a blueprint is excellent, but you must commit to a deadline in order to see your plan become a reality. Henry Ford said it best: "Vision without execution is just hallucination."[1]

Henry Ford said it best: "Vision without execution is just hallucination."[1]

Are you ready to get started building your plan from the blueprint you created? As mentioned earlier, you need to create a "do list". DO means DO! This is an action plan; therefore it is time to take action!

Here are some action steps that can help make your financial plan become a reality:

Secure Your Income

Once you have decided what your best earning potential is, begin to move toward that goal. Income planning is paramount in the success of your overall plan. If you are still in the workforce and are happy with your current situation, perhaps there is nothing more to be done in this area for now.

However, if you want to change positions, you must begin taking action steps toward that end. Perhaps there is an opening at your present workplace that pays more money than your current position. If you feel like it would be a positive move for you, be aggressive in securing that position. Initiate a meeting with the person in charge and tell him or her why you are perfect for the opening. Be bold! Most employers like it when an employee shows interest in moving up within the company.

Maybe you have decided that you want to establish a business; if so, you must begin taking steps to make that decision become a reality instead of a dream. Bookstore shelves are lined with books on how to start your own business. Pick up a book or two on the subject. The $20 or $40 you spend on the books will be your first investment toward your new business. Remember, taking a first step is very empowering.

Income planning will also be an important step for a person who is no longer in the workforce. More than likely your income will come from investments. Begin to compile a list of every asset and account you have that could be used for income. Make sure that your plan includes income for the present as well as the future.

Organize

Organization will also be a key step toward implementing your plan. Remember, you must establish your Point A before moving toward your Point B. Not knowing your current location can debilitate a financial plan before it even gets started. Many women have piles of unorganized statements that have built up over the years. The task of sorting through them may seem daunting, but dive in and do the best you can. More than likely you will decide many of them need to go to the shredder.

Organizing your portfolio is much like organizing your closet. Deciding what you need to keep and what you should get rid of is normally the first step. Once that is done it will be much easier to organize what is left because you will know what you have to work with. If you decide to meet with a financial adviser, you will have at least established your starting point. Most advisers are willing to help with the organizational process, so do the best you can before your initial meeting and then allow the adviser to help with the rest. Just like cleaning out a closet, together, you will decide what is outdated or no longer a good fit for you.

Most women feel better immediately once things get organized. Everyone knows how great it feels to walk into a freshly organized closet; there is a certain calmness and sense of achievement simply because order has been established. The stress that was created when muddling through an unorganized mess has been eliminated.

When women put off organizing their closets, their portfolio or their life in general, they can waste hours, days, months or even years trying to sort through the mess. Don't be a procrastinator. Take an action step and begin now to organize your statements, legal documents, etc., so that you can easily establish your Point A.

Find Professionals

Once you have done everything you can on your own, chances are you will need to seek the advice and assistance of professionals such as a financial adviser, an insurance agent, a CPA and/or an attorney. Here are some things to consider when meeting with such advisers:

1) Find out what part of your plan they are able to help you with. The products and services they offer will vary.

2) Pay very close attention to how much attention the adviser is paying to you! Good advisers will be very interested in what you have to say. They will ask questions to make sure they have a good understanding of your current situation, as well as your goals. If you meet with someone who can't stop talking about what he or she can do for you without first hearing what your needs are, they are likely more interested in meeting their own goals than yours.

3) Good advisers will take the time to educate you to the best of their ability about the subject at hand. They will want to help you understand your options so that you are equipped to make good decisions.

4) Professionals are paid in a variety of ways; some charge fees for their services while others make a commission on products. While there are many opinions on this subject, I personally do not think it matters how or what they get paid. The question is, can they help you get into a more favorable financial position?

5) If you are married and meet with a professional with your husband, notice how much the person focuses his or her attention on you. I have heard many women complain about the fact that some advisers spend entire meetings looking and speaking to their husbands only, barely even glancing their way or acknowledging their presence in the room. Sometimes this has happened even when the women held most of the assets in their names! Make sure your adviser spends ample time addressing both of you. If an adviser is not paying enough attention to you now, he or she may not pay you any attention later if your husband predeceases you.

If you are going to need the services of any professional to help with your financial or estate plan, do not put it off. Make an appointment and keep it. When you find a professional you are comfortable with, continue making follow-up appointments until your plan is complete.

Pick Your Investments

Choosing the right investments for building your plan is extremely important. Here are a few things to consider:

1) If you have not yet retired, decide how much you can contribute to a retirement plan. Putting money aside for the future can be hard, but it is a must for securing your future

income. Decide which plan is best for you. If your employer is willing to match your investment, that is an excellent place to start.

2) Perhaps you would also like to invest in real estate. To be a smart real estate investor, you must do your homework; search out properties that have good income potential without being a constant drain on your pocketbook for repairs. In addition, you will need to decide whether you want to be a direct landlord or hire a service to manage the property for you.

3) Market investments can be a wise choice if you can tolerate the risk and have the proper time horizon. You must decide how much you can afford to risk, and when you will need the funds. As I mentioned earlier, age matters and must be taken into consideration as you pick investments. As with real estate, purchasing and managing stocks, bonds and mutual funds can be done directly, or you may want to pay a professional to manage the investments for you. Many people do very well handling their own investments, while others suffer great losses.

Purchase Insurance Products

Chances are you may need one or more insurance products: life insurance, annuities and/or long-term care. Consider what type of protection you need:

1) Review the many uses for life insurance described in chapter 12. You may have the need for coverage on yourself or someone else. Learn the difference between term, whole life and universal life insurance. A financial adviser or life

insurance agent can explain how each one works and suggest the one that best fits your needs.

2) Perhaps annuities are a good fit for you. Today's versions of annuities can offer many types of protection and benefits, including lifetime income and tax-deferral. Some annuities have income riders that guarantee a certain amount of growth for the value used to calculate income. Some annuities even offer nursing home benefits.

3) Long-term care should be considered if you are middle-aged or beyond. You must weigh the benefits offered through various policies. Cost of insurance as well as benefits should be thoroughly understood before purchasing a policy. If you decide that long-term care insurance is appropriate for your situation, do your homework and choose a policy that works for you.

Minimize Taxes

As you pick investments and insurance products, be aware of the tax situations with each:

1) Putting money in qualified accounts, such as a 401k, 403b, SEP, IRA, etc. will allow you to defer paying taxes on the initial investment as well as the growth.

2) For additional tax planning, you may need to choose tax-free or tax-deferred vehicles.

To build a strong plan, the tax status of your investments will be a very important consideration. Make sure you don't find yourself with an uncoordinated plan, where the returns on your investments are eaten up by taxes that may even include your Social Security being taxed unnecessarily.

The professionals who assist you with choosing investments and insurance products can help explain the taxation of each. A CPA can help you with filing your taxes and may suggest strategies that can lower your tax bill; however, most CPAs spend their time trying to stay current on tax laws. Many women make the mistake of thinking CPAs are financial advisers; while some are, most are not.

Complete an Estate Plan

Remember, if you own something, you have an estate. The amount of estate planning you will need to do will be based on the types of assets you have. However, here are some suggestions that may help:

1) Begin with simple things like confirming the beneficiaries of your retirement accounts and insurance contracts.

2) For other accounts, such as bank and brokerage accounts, you may want to list a POD (Payable on Death) or TOD (Transfer on Death) for your desired beneficiaries. This is an extremely easy process and can keep these accounts from being probated at your death. The other way these accounts can be set up is to have them owned by your trust.

3) Get your legal documents in order. Speak to an attorney and decide which route is best for you to most efficiently pass your assets to heirs. He or she may suggest a will or a trust. This normally depends on the type of assets you have, as well as the state in which you live. In addition, most attorneys will

recommend documents such as a Power of Attorney for Asset Management, a Health Care Directive and a Living Will.

Make sure you have a clear understanding of the attorney's fees. Find out if there is an hourly rate or a one-time fee based on the size of the project. In addition, find out if there are charges for making changes and amendments to documents in the future.

Implementing your plan before something becomes a crisis is very important. Make it a priority. Waiting until you are in panic mode or have an emergency could be too little, too late. Move your plan along with tenacity. Don't allow distractions to derail you. Constantly take steps toward completing your plan. Before you know it, you will have a strong tower that will shelter you and your family from life's storms and maximize your financial portfolio.

CHAPTER SUMMARY

1) Secure Your Income

   - Promotion at work

   - Establish a business

   - Maximize your investments

2) Organize

   - Sort through your piles

   - Decide what needs to be kept and what doesn't

   - Allow your adviser to help

3) Find Professionals

   - Financial adviser, insurance agent, CPA, attorney

   - Are they paying attention?

   - Educate you about your options

   - Payment

4) Pick Your Investments

   - Retirement accounts

   - Real estate

- Market

5) Purchase Insurance Products

   - Determine your needs

   - Life insurance, annuities, long-term care

6) Minimize Taxes

   - Deferred qualified accounts

   - Deferred nonqualified accounts

7) Complete an Estate Plan

   - Review beneficiaries

   - POD (Payable on Death) and TOD (Transfer on Death)

   - Will, Trust, Power of Attorney, Health Care Directive, Living Will

   - Attorney's fees

CHAPTER 14

Results of a Good P.L.A.N.

People don't plan to fail; they fail to plan. Women who understand the importance of financial planning will take the necessary steps to secure their financial future. Ask yourself the following questions:

- Am I maximizing my income opportunities?

- Am I investing for the future?

- Have I protected my assets?

- Are my legal documents in order?

- Do I feel financially secure?

- Do I have a plan?

If you are not able to answer yes to all of these questions, you should take the appropriate steps to change that. As you build your financial plan, you will begin to feel financially secure. Trust me, the time and effort you spend designing and building the plan will be well worth it. Please allow me to give you one final acronym that describes what a good Financial P.L.A.N. will do for you.

People don't plan to fail;
they fail to plan.

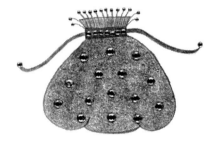

Power to control your financial future

While many things in life cannot be controlled, having a strong financial plan will certainly empower you to deal with whatever financial situations may come your way. Leaving your finances to chance is like being on a ship with no one at the helm. The ship will drift around, being influenced by whatever wind or storm it encounters. Left to guide itself, the ship may crash or even sink.

By getting your finances in order and staying in control, you will be able to stay on course and ultimately reach your desired destination.

Leverage to be used when needed

Being able to maneuver through life's financial storms is critical. A woman who has taken the time to get her financial household in order will find that she has the leverage to steer through these rough waters. She will have created for herself and her family a significant tool for staying in control of the situation.

Because she has prepared for what may lie ahead, her strong financial plan will give her the power she needs to deal with each circumstance. She will not be overtaken when financial storms come.

Accurate picture of where you are, where you are going and how you will get there

When planning a trip, one must know the starting point, the destination and the best means for getting there. A well-designed financial plan will enable you to clearly understand your current situation, articulate your goals and dreams and decide what vehicles you need for reaching them.

New level of confidence and peace of mind

Confidence is a powerful word. Joyce Meyer wrote a fantastic book I would highly recommend, *The Confident Woman*.[1] In this book, she addresses the reasons women often lack confidence and what they must do to address this issue.

Women who take the time to deal with their financial and estate plans will find a new level of confidence they may never have experienced before. This will most likely spill over into other areas of their lives, giving them the boldness to face each issue head on and make necessary changes for living life at its best.

Taking the time to build and implement a good plan can save you years of agony. Instead of going through life with your head covered, you will be able to boldly march forward, ready for whatever may come your way. Which position do you prefer?

Worry and the stress of not knowing where you are, how you will deal with the future and where you may wind up will take a huge toll on you over the years. However, a woman who has built a strong plan will be confident knowing that she will be able to handle whatever financial storm life may toss her way. The peace of mind she possesses is invaluable!

WHAT DO YOU HAVE IN YOUR FINANCIAL PURSE TODAY?

Is your purse filled with unnecessary items, or does it contain all you need to secure your financial future? If it does, its contents will consist of the many items we addressed throughout this book. Let's do a quick review, beginning with the **P.U.R.S.E.S.** acronym:

PURPOSE BASED PLANNING: Having a plan that is based around an intended or desired result to meet the particular needs of the individual.

UNDERSTANDING MONEY BASICS: Having a basic understanding of how money works, how it grows and how to handle money on a day-to-day basis.

RESOURCES AVAILABLE: Being aware of the various investment options and products that are available to you for building your Purpose Based Plan.

STAGES OF LIFE: The four financial stages of life: accumulation, distribution, preservation and transfer.

EMPOWERED FOR DECISION MAKING: Having the necessary knowledge and experience to make proper decisions regarding your finances and estate plan.

SECURITY SYSTEM FOR YOUR ASSETS: Understanding all of the predators that can cause unnecessary loss to your assets and setting up a system for protection against them.

By having the right contents in your financial purse, you will most likely be able to:

- Reach the five basic financial goals: financial success, financial freedom, financial responsibility, financial independence and financial security.

- Cast aside money myths, enabling you to deal with what is real and what isn't.

- Create a productive money garden, providing all you need for the present and enough to preserve for the future.

- Avoid financial mistakes, saving yourself and your family from unnecessary loss, stress and worry.

- Have an overall strong financial plan: a written plan, an updated plan, a coordinated plan, the right plan, a complete plan, an implemented plan, a flexible plan and a plan that works for both life and death.

- Maximize your income plan: having all the income you need for the present, as well as during your retirement years.

- Have the best tax plan, reducing your tax liability by creating tax-deferred accounts and eliminating unnecessary overpayment of taxes.

- Leave a legacy through your estate plan that will maximize the amount your heirs will receive from the estate you leave behind and minimize the time, complication and stress associated with settling the estate.

A purse is a very personal item for a woman. The outside may reflect her style or personality; however, the inside of the purse holds what is valuable to her. How much value do you place on your financial future and that of your loved ones? Is it worth taking a little time and effort to get things in order?

If so, I hope the suggestions, ideas, examples and tools in this book will help you reach your goals. My desire is that you will be motivated to take care of one of the most important areas in or life: your finances.

CHAPTER SUMMARY

A good financial P.L.A.N.

- **P**ower to control your financial future

- **L**everage to be used when needed

- **A**ccurate picture of where you are, where you are going and how you will get there

- **N**ew level of confidence and peace of mind.

Having the right contents in your purse will allow you to:

- reach the five basic financial goals

- cast aside money myths

- create a productive money garden

- avoid financial mistakes

- have an overall strong financial plan

- maximize income

- have the best tax plan

- leave a legacy through your estate plan

CHAPTER 15

Giving Back

You will notice that throughout this book I have not given advice on specific investments, nor have I taken you down the complicated road of tax laws. My intention was to give you a roadmap for developing a plan, not to try to turn you into a financial adviser, CPA or attorney overnight. These professionals train for years to gain the knowledge needed for their specific fields, and they are available to assist you in customizing your plan.

However, I *would* like to tell you what I believe is the best investment you will ever make, and that is the investment you make in others. I am a firm believer in what goes around comes around.

Winston Churchill is supposed to have said, "We make a living by what we get, but we make a life by what we give."[1] A person can possess great wealth, but if she does not have purpose and an outlet for giving, she will still feel the pains of emptiness.

I believe that living life to the fullest requires extending a hand to others. When a ship is sinking, there are those who are in the lifeboat and those who are in the water. Normally, those who have made it to safety in the lifeboat will extend a hand to those who are still in the water. Which position would you rather be in?

"We make a living by what we get, but we make a life by what we give."[1]

Throughout life, people will most likely find themselves in both of these situations at one time or another. Many of life's circumstances require us to reach out for help, and there is nothing wrong with that. A person who refuses help from another will sometimes drown due to her own pride or stubbornness. Don't be afraid to reach out for help when in need: financially, physically, emotionally or spiritually.

With that said, we should do everything possible to position ourselves to be the one to extend the helping hand. That means we must first secure ourselves. If you have ever flown on a commercial flight, you've heard the announcement made in regard to the oxygen masks: secure your own mask first before assisting others. If you lose consciousness trying to help someone else, chances are your efforts will be futile. In the same way, a person who is drowning is not in the position to help someone else safely to shore.

When we have secured ourselves first, we will be in a much better position to reach out to others. When someone has a financial need, we will be able to reach into our purse to find there is enough there to be shared.

Of course, helping someone financially is only one way of reaching out to them. Giving of our time and energy can be just as important. Look around you; who do you see that could use your assistance in some way? Whose life can you affect in a positive way by extending a helping hand to them? The opportunities are everywhere.

Make a conscious effort to reach out to others as often as you can. There are many strategies you can use that will help with this:

- Make a list of people and organizations that would benefit greatly from your help. You will want to focus on those who you are not enabling to be overly dependent on you.

- Try reaching out to at least one person each day. This could mean something as small as helping an elderly person cross the street or assisting a young mother who is trying to load groceries in the car while dealing with her small children. Sometimes just uttering a few kind words to the waitress, cashier or taxi cab driver has a bigger impact than you think.

- Keep a journal of your good deeds. This does not mean you are cocky or prideful; instead, it will help you realize how much you have to offer others. Once you've seen the positive effect you've had on people, your life will seem fuller and much more satisfying.

I encourage you to take the necessary steps to be responsible with your own life so that you will be in a position to know the joy of reaching out to others. Henry Ford said, "To do more for the world than the world does for you – that is success."[2]

The world has many definitions for success, including fame, money and power. While these may be results of your achievements in the world, make sure you keep them in their proper place. Do not allow them to define you. Instead, be known as a confident, responsible woman who takes care of her own affairs, as well as making a difference in the lives of others. This will allow you to be become the best version of yourself in this world.

CHAPTER SUMMARY

- The best investment you will ever make is in the lives of others.

- Secure yourself so that you will be in a position to help others.

- Give more than you take.

- A confident, responsible woman who reaches out to others will become the best version of herself.

NOTES

Chapter 2

1. National Education and Resource Center on Women and Retirement Planning
http://www.wiserwomen.org
2. The Department of Health and Human Services, Administration on Aging, http://www.aoa.gov/AoARoot/Aging_Statistics/Profile/2013/2.aspx
3. Women Talk Money, http://www.womentalkmoney.com/Stats.html
4. National Education and Resource Center on Women and Retirement Planning
http://www.wiserwomen.org
5. The Department of Health and Human Services, Administration on Aging, http://www.aoa.gov/AoARoot/Aging_Statistics/Profile/2013/2.aspx
6. Women Talk Money, http://www.womentalkmoney.com/Stats.html
7. Divorce Statistics, http://www.divorcestatistics.org/
8. National Education and Resource Center on Women and Retirement Planning http://www.wiserwomen.org
9. Susan Brown, BGSU: The Gray Divorce Revolution: Rising Divorce among Middle-aged and Older Adults, 1990-2009, http://ipr.osu.edu/events/susan-brown-bgsu-gray-divorce-revolution-rising-divorce-among-middle-aged-and-older-adults-19

10. The Department of Health and Human Services, Administration on Aging, http://www.aoa.gov/AoARoot/Aging_Statistics/Profile/2013/5.aspx

11. National Center for Family and Marriage Research at Bowling Green State University http://www.bgsu.edu/arts-and-sciences/center-for-family-demographic-research.html

12. The Department of Health and Human Services, Administration on Aging, http://www.aoa.gov/AoARoot/Aging_Statistics/Profile/2013/6.aspx

13. Ibid.

14. Women Talk Money, http://www.womentalkmoney.com/Stats.html

15. Women & Money Magazine, http://womenmoneyandsuccessmag.com/resources/statistics

16. National Center for Women and Retirement Research (NCWRR)

17. Ibid.

18. Women & Money Magazine, http://womenmoneyandsuccessmag.com/resources/statistics

19. National Education and Resource Center on Women and Retirement Planning, http://www.wiserwomen.org

20. US Census Bureau

21. National Education and Resource Center on Women and Retirement Planning, http://www.wiserwomen.org

22. Ibid.

23. National Center for Women and Retirement Research, http://www.worknwoman.com/worknmom/finance/finance_main.html

24. Ibid.

25. Niles Williamson, "Increasing Number of US Seniors Living In Poverty" 26 March 2013 http://www.wsws.org/en/articles/2013/03/26/seni-m26.html

26. Ibid.

27. Ibid.

28. Employee Benefit Research Institute, http://www.ebri.org/publications/facts/

29. MetLife Mature Market Institute, https://www.metlife.com/assets/cao/mmi/publications/studies/2012/studies/mmi-2012-market-survey-long-term-care-costs.pdf

30. Grabstats.com, http://www.grabstats.com/statmain.aspx?Stat ID=1324

31. Employee Benefit Research Institute, http://www.ebri.org/publications/facts/

32. MetLife Mature Market Institute, https://www.metlife.com/assets/cao/mmi/publications/studies/2012/studies/mmi-2012-market-survey-long-term-care-costs.pdf

33. Ibid.

34. U.S. Department of Health and Human Services, http://longtermcare.gov/

35. Ibid.

36. Ibid.

Chapter 3

1. http://www.brainyquote.com/quotes/quotes/h/henryford122817.html

2. http://www.goodreads.com/author/quotes/85179.Lou_Holtz

3. John C. Maxwell, *The Difference Maker: Making Your Attitude Your Greatest Asset* (Nashville, TN: Thomas Nelson, 2006), 45

4. Random Facts, "Twenty Facts About Millionaires and Billionaires"

5. http://facts.randomhistory.com/millionaires-facts.html. http://www.goodreads.com/author/quotes/85179.Lou_Holtz

Chapter 4

1. http://www.usdebtclock.org/
2. http://facts.randomhistory.com/debt-crisis-facts.html
Copyright ©2007-2014 Random History.com
3. Ibid.
4. The Bible, New International Version, I Timothy 6:10

Chapter 5

1. Robert Kiyosaki, *Rich Dad's Cashflow Quadrant: Rich Dad's Guide to Financial Freedom* (Scottsdale, AZ: Plata Publishing, LLC, 1998)
2. Random Facts, "Twenty Facts About Millionaires and Billionaires"
http://facts.randomhistory.com/millionaires-facts.html.
Copyright ©2007-2014 Random History.com
3. http://www.salary.com/2013-mom-infographics/
4. *Keep Calm and Carry On; Advice for Hard Times* (Kansas City, MO: Andrews McMeel
Publishing, LLC, 2009)
5. http://facts.randomhistory.com/debt-crisis-facts.html

Chapter 6

1. *Keep Calm and Carry On; Advice for Hard Times* (Kansas City, MO: Andrews McMeel
Publishing, LLC, 2009).
2. Ibid.
3. Ibid.
4. http://facts.randomhistory.com/debt-crisis-facts.html

Chapter 8

1. http://www.working.com/vancouver/resources/2006super section/story.html?id=5f4de417-a881-471b-be2b-9f539f 8501a9&p=2
2. http://money.usnews.com/money/blogs/the-best-life/2013/ 03/08/13-social-security-planning-questions

Chapter 9

1. Death and Taxes, The Public Square Transcript http://www.aproundtable.org/tps30info/taxes.html
2. http://facts.randomhistory.com/debt-crisis-facts.html
3. http://www.facts.randomhistory.com/tax-facts.html
4. Ibid.

Chapter 11

1. Bruce Wilkinson, *Dream Giver* (Sisters, OR: Multnomah Publishers, 2003)
2. http://www.goodreads.com/author/quotes/85179.Lou_Holtz

Chapter 13

1. http://www.brainyquote.com/quotes/quotes/h/henryford 122817.html

Chapter 14

[1.] Joyce Meyer, *The Confident Woman* (New York, NY: Warner Faith Hachette Book Group, 2006)

Chapter 15

[1.] *Keep Calm and Carry On; Advice for Hard Times* (Kansas City, MO: Andrews McMeel Publishing, LLC, 2009).

[2.] http://www.brainyquote.com/quotes/quotes/h/henryford 122817.html

ABOUT THE AUTHOR

Bobbie Messmore has been licensed in the financial services industry for over ten years. She is an award-winning adviser and 2014 member of the Million Dollar Round Table (MDRT), The Premier Association of Financial Professionals.®

Bobbie is the president of Strategic Planning Masters, LLC, a financial planning company, as well as PALS Link, LLC, a marketing company. She is the founder of an organization for women, The JEWELS, which is an acronym for Joyous, Energetic Women Embracing Life. The JEWELS consists of thousands of female members and promotes financial security, health and fitness and emotional and spiritual wellness among women.

Bobbie is the author and speaker of the popular financial workshop, P.U.R.S.E.S. This workshop has been presented to thousands of females across the country by top financial advisers.

Bobbie lives in Tampa, FL, with her husband, Thomas.

The JEWELS is an organization for women founded by Bobbie Messmore. For more information, or to order additional copies of the P.U.R.S.E.S. book, please visit the website.

Joyous Energetic Women Embracing Life

MISSION STATEMENT

The JEWELS organization promotes financial security, health & fitness, and emotional and spiritual wellness for the unique needs of women. The fundamental purpose of The JEWELS organization is to provide opportunities for women to understand their value and reach their potential success in each of these areas. Through workshops, conventions, social gatherings and many forms of media, resources are made available to instruct and encourage women to "sparkle and shine" as they embrace all that life has to offer.

Website:
www.thejewels.org

Go to The JEWELS website to learn more about financial services, workshops and professionals who may be able to assist you with Financial and Estate Planning.

CPSIA information can be obtained at www.ICGtesting.com
Printed in the USA
LVOW11*1238231014

410098LV00001B/4/P

9 781490 742830